What others are sayin

Interpreting the characteristics common to all empires and locating our place in the cycle of their ascendency and decline is not an easy task. We can thank Bill Goetz for helping us see that events in North America—particularly the United States—lead us to believe that we just might be on our last gasp; judgment might well be on the way. What shall we do about it? Goetz points out that our only hope is a return to the gospel, lived out by believers and shared with the world. Read this book for understanding; then share it with others.

Dr. Erwin Lutzer,
Pastor Moody Church, Chicago

Centuries ago Confucius wrote, "Study the past if you would divine the future." More recently George Santayana sounded the warning, "Those who cannot remember the past are condemned to fulfil it." Goetz has given us a portrait of civilization's past that serves as a mirror for our times. . . . If he is right, as I believe he is, the West is doomed to come under God's righteous judgment. . . . Just as God through His servant Jeremiah directed the attention of of His people to His judgment on Shiloh, so through this biblical analysis of the rise and fall of great empires of the past he calls us to consider just where we might be on the slippery slope that leads to ruin. But Goetz does not leave us there: he points us to the Christian's hope that God's kingdom will yet be established on earth in power and glory.

Dr. Ted S. Rendall
Chancellor Emeritus, Prairie Bible College
Author, *Fire in the Church*

*In this thought-provoking survey of the rise and fall of past civiliza-
tions, Goetz identifies warning signs suggesting a coming collapse of
the American "empire" in the twenty-first century.*

Dr. William B. Bedford
Professor of History, Crown College
St. Bonifacius, Minnesota

When the Empire Strikes Out *is a fascinating and important read. This
is no doomsday diatribe, but a perceptive analysis of world history
combined with a clarion call for change—one that must echo loudly
down the corridors of a culture in decline. Bill Goetz does more than
just paint a vivid word picutre of this society's sunset years. He writes
across the canvas in vivid colors a beautiful word: Hope.*

Phil Callaway, Editor, *Servant Magazine*,
Author of *Making Life Rich Without Any Money*
and *I Used to Have Answers . . . Now I Have Kids*

When the Empire Strikes Out *is the most convincing wake-up call I
have seen during my lifetime. It cannot be summarily dimissed as just
one more religious fanatic "crying wolf." This book argues from a
long history of secular academic research done by responsible historians.*

Dr. Arnold Cook, Author, *Historical Drift*

WHEN THE EMPIRE STRIKES OUT

When the Empire Strikes Out

Are we repeating the pattern of past civilizations?

William R. Goetz

HORIZON BOOKS

A division of Christian Publications, Inc.

CAMP HILL, PENNSYLVANIA

HORIZON BOOKS

A division of Christian Publications, Inc.
3825 Hartzdale Drive
Camp Hill, PA 17011
www.cpi-horizon.com
www.christianpublications.com

When the Empire Strikes Out
ISBN: 0-88965-184-1

LOC Control Number: 2001-130450

© 2001 by Horizon Books

Contents

Foreword   ix

Preface   xi

Introduction   xiii

Part One: *Here an Empire,*
There an Empire, Everywhere an Empire

1 Empires in "Galaxies Far, Far Away,"
Times Long, Long Ago—and Today   1

Part Two: *Sir John Finds a Pattern*

2 Meet Sir John Glubb   9

3 The Fate of Empires   13

4 A Valid View?   25

5 When in Rome . . .   39

Part Three: *Will History Repeat Itself? (Maybe)*

6 Take, for Example, the United States   61

7 Women—Equal or Superior?   81

8 Our Star-Studded Heroes   93

9 In Addition to Which . . .   113

10 Twenty-First Century Barbarians   137

Part Four: Is the Empire of Man Striking Out?

11 The Futurists: Gloomy and Otherwise   153

12 The Biblical Prophecies   167

Part Five: How Then Shall We Live?

13 Lifestyles of the Wise and the Unwise   187

14 The Normal Christian Life   201

Epilogue: And He Shall Reign   209

Proclamation of President Bush's
National Day of Prayer and Thanksgiving   213

Selected Bibliography   215

Scripture Index   221

Subject Index   227

Foreword

A full life of seventy years has taught me that in choosing the books I read, the author is usually more important than the topic. Whereas in this case the topic is also both vital and compelling reading, it is still very much because of the author that I feel honored to have been asked to write this foreword.

Bill Goetz is deeply respected by those who know him. His genuine humility in always seeking to shift the spotlight from himself to others is a widely recognized trademark, along with his gentle spirit.

He has done a superb job with *When the Empire Strikes Out*. His patience in research seems unlimited, and he has spared no effort in presenting the facts as objectively and truthfully as possible.

It has been well noted that what we learn from history is that we rarely learn from history. Yet, if our current warped, anemic and totally inadequate understanding of "learning" is the mere accumulating of facts so as to store them in minds or computers, we certainly do learn—and learn lots. But let us not be fooled. For our problem is, as Glubb Pasha noted, that we stop at the cerebral. The need to actually do something about it by bringing our lives into line scarcely crosses our minds. As in many areas of modern-day Christianity, we have substituted the understanding of the concept for the experiencing of the reality.

Bill has obviously been motivated by the longing that this timely book will not just inform our minds but activate our wills. Although we may not altogether prevent the Glubb cycle from being repeated, we can realistically aim at delaying as long as possible the deteriorating descent from the valuable "doing" stage to the merely "knowing" stage.

These insightful chapters are well worth re-probing slowly after the initial reading. And as well as merely learning the lesson ourselves, we would do well to try and place a copy of this unique book into the hands of key national and community leaders. What a giant leap for mankind if we could see it pronounced "required reading" for all those entering any form of public office.

Thank you, Bill, for doing us all the great favor of guiding us through this life-changing and unusual approach to learning from history.

Keith A. Price
Minister-at-Large
The Evangelical Fellowship of Canada
October 2000

Preface

Until recently I have not had a compelling interest in history. To be sure, I had some degree of awareness that history has valuable lessons to teach us, lessons which we seldom seem willing to learn. As Hegel once remarked, "What experience and history teach us is this—that people and government never have learned anything from history, or acted on principles deduced from it."[1]

I was also familiar with the statement that "those who fail to learn from the mistakes of history are condemned to repeat them." Nevertheless, I was not "into" history. My interests lay in the study of prophecy—the future, not the past.

My awakening to the value of history came some years ago in the midst of a lecture by Dr. Keith Price during a three-day retreat for pastors and their wives held in the winter off-season at a Canadian resort. In the course of his lecture Dr. Price referred to a recently deceased military man and avid historian who had made some fascinating observations based on a study of 4,000 years of human history. Sir John Glubb, said Dr. Price, had identified certain characteristics common to all empires which in timing and effect were virtually identical throughout each empire's course from inception to collapse.

I was intrigued.

I reasoned, along with Dr. Price, that if Sir John's thesis was correct, it would be possible through an identification of our culture's characteristics to have an informed idea about where we are in the life cycle of the empire we know as the United States of America. The same would hold true, of course, for Canada, her northerly neighbor and earnest imitator.

Subsequent thought, study and research lit a spark in me, a spark that continues to unfold as an ever-increasing fascination. It has also strengthened my conviction that a comparison of past and current cultures may have significant lessons for us in the future. More than that, the fascination has resulted in this volume, offered for the reader's thoughtful consideration near the outset of a new millennium.

I would be seriously remiss if I failed to express my appreciation to the late Dr. Keith Price and acknowledge the role he has played in my journey. Not only did he initially pique my interest, but he also subsequently provided encouragement and other valuable resources along the way. A respected administrator, pastor, preacher, author and lecturer in Canada for more than half a century, Dr. Price, who passed away in early 2001, was a valued friend whose leadership was widely recognized.

Thus, if *When the Empire Strikes Out* proves to be of value, Dr. Price must share the credit, as must also Dr. K. Neill Foster, President/Publisher of Christian Publications, Inc., for his friendship and encouragement to put these concepts into writing.

Endnote
1. G.W.F. Hegel, *Philosophy of History*, quoted in *The Oxford Dictionary of Quotations, Third Edition* (New York, NY: Oxford University Press, 1980), 244.

Introduction

Is the human race on a collision course with global disaster? A growing number of alarmists seem to think so. And thoughtful people are full of questions:

> Do the predictions of numerous and apparently credible doomsayers from a variety of disciplines have any validity?
>
> What of the fearful forecasts of global environmental collapse?
>
> Are the planet's natural resources, so essential to our survival, actually going to run out?
>
> Can the growing tendency to violence on the part of both individuals and nations be curbed?
>
> Is it possible to eliminate the curse of ethnic hatred and cleansing?
>
> Is there hope for mankind in a world that possesses sufficient weapons of mass destruction to literally annihilate the human race?
>
> Is the "empire of man" about to strike out?

The purpose of this book is to respond to these and similar questions through an examination of secular history and biblical prophecy, as well as the writings of futurists and theologians. A balanced, though admittedly sobering conclusion—tempered with a message of genuine hope—is offered the serious reader.

I invite you to examine the evidence presented here and draw your own conclusions.

Here an Empire,
There an Empire,
Everywhere an Empire

Empire. The word has different meaning for different people. For a majority of North Americans, especially children and youth, the term most likely creates visions of *Star Wars*—Darth Vader, Luke, The Force—and all of the numerous characters who people this enormously popular fictional and futuristic struggle between good and evil.

But for business people, politicians or historians, the word "empire" may conjure up in each case a radically different image.

In Part One, we'll look briefly at the various versions of the term "empire" and define its use for our understanding in the following pages.

Chapter One

Empires in "Galaxies Far, Far Away," Times Long, Long Ago—and Today

The Soviet Union is an evil empire. . . .
It is destined to failure.

—U.S. President Ronald Reagan,
in a speech to the British House of Commons,
March 8, 1983

It was called "empire mania." Fueled by the release of *Star Wars Episode 1: The Phantom Menace,* interest in the concept of "empire" reached fever pitch. In cities across the country, young people camped out in front of movie theaters in line ups that formed as early as a month before the scheduled May 1999 release of the new film. The camp outs created bizarre scenes, with fans dressed like aliens, princesses and Jedi knights. Accompanied by lawn chairs, sleeping bags, ice chests, portable TVs and laptop computers, many hardcore *Star Wars* devo-

1

tees obviously expected the massive effort to get into the first showing of the new series to be worthwhile.

The first *Star Wars* movie, which came out in 1977, broke new ground in special effects and high-tech movie making. The other films in the initial trilogy, *The Empire Strikes Back* and *The Return of the Jedi*, helped usher in what some have called a "new culture of good versus evil," and in the process created an almost cult-like following. Thus, millions fantasize about the high-tech struggle "in a galaxy far, far away" between medieval imperial hierarchies with their nobility, princes and emperors.

The series also embodied spiritual issues. The *Star Wars* bad guys downplayed "The Force" as merely a superstition, while the cassock-clad Jedi knights were warrior-monks who tapped into The Force's supernatural power. Although vaguely reminiscent of God, The Force was impersonal and had both a good and evil, light and dark side in direct contrast to the God of the Bible.

The initial *Star Wars* trilogy posited an evil empire, which, like the Soviet Union under President Reagan's Star Wars defense, was defeated. Consequently, with its superb story-telling appeal and groundbreaking special effects, the *Star Wars* series imparted to the children and youth of its generation—whom it obviously targeted—a concept of empire which would perhaps otherwise be unknown.

The term "empire" has, of course, been used in reference to many other entities, most of them far more significant than the fictional *Star Wars* domains, even with the series' acknowledged impact on North American culture.

Check It Out for Yourself

Historically, as we shall see in succeeding chapters, the account of the human race is full of the exploits, excesses and legacies—for good or bad—of a parade of empires, many of which historians have termed "great." The gore and glories of these empires, such as Egypt, Assyria, Babylon, Persia, Greece, Rome and others, fill the pages of countless history books. Without dispute, each of these ancient cultures has in one way or another left its indelible mark on the present era.

The mid-twentieth century saw the decline of the once-powerful British Empire begun in the 1700s with its "Rule Britannica" mind-set and the factual boast that the sun never set on its far-flung armies, navies, colonies and outposts around the globe.

The account of the human race is full of the exploits, excesses and legacies— for good or bad—of a parade of empires.

A 1917 revolution launched communism into a seventy-year empire that brought enslavement and death to multiplied millions of earth's peoples.

The 1930s saw the rise of the ill-fated and destructive Thousand-Year Reich (read "Empire") of Adolf Hitler which resulted in World War II during which 50 million soldiers and civilians perished before the insane dream of Hitler's empire was finally defeated in 1945.

Though it did not arrive at its status in the usual fashion, nonetheless the United States is unquestionably an empire in the basic sense of the word. With the defeat and breakup of the Soviet Union—called the "evil empire" by President Reagan—the United States now stands as the last remaining superpower, a term used interchangeably with "empire."

Break Up Microsoft!

The business world, too, is and has been filled with empires.

The closing days of the twentieth century saw a mighty struggle between the U.S. government, with its claim that Microsoft was a monopoly, and Bill Gates, CEO and multibillionaire founder of the computer software giant. At the time of this writing, the courts had ordered the breakup of Gates' empire, a decision which was being appealed. The action served as a reminder of the previous court-ordered breakup of another U.S. business empire when Bell Telephone—"Ma Bell"—was forced to split into a number of "Baby Bells."

The roll call of international business conglomerates, which in a very real sense could be described as financial empires, has in recent decades become an extensive listing. Increasingly, multinational corporations have the look and power of bona fide empires. Many have financial resources that far exceed the Gross National Product (GNP) totals of a majority of nations.

Disney Rules

In the entertainment world, one entity stands out with empire status. The Disney Corporation, with its various movie companies, multiplying complexes on several continents, video, television, music and publishing companies, as well as a variety of related holdings, is unquestionably an enormous empire. And other entertainment/communications giants with far-reaching influence also wield the degree of power that makes the term "empire" entirely appropriate. Mergers, takeovers and fierce battles for the control of companies are all part of the normal course of events in the never-ending realm of empire building—events which I believe are obvious indications of a world in constant flux.

In this ever-changing era, business empires don't last. The history of the business world is strewn with the wreckage, or at best the pitiful remains, of once-powerful empires. Railroad barons are no more—just one example among many which could be cited.

But business empires aren't the only ones that don't last. Political machines (empires) break down; sports dynasties and their "emperors" fade; investment empires disappear overnight (some emperors even go to jail); and, as history abundantly illustrates, once-mighty national powers wither and decay.

Life Cycle of an Empire

Since the evidence appears to indicate clearly that no empire of any genus lasts forever, the questions arise: Are there characteristics which mark the various stages in the life cycle of an empire? Is it possible to know when an empire is winding down and facing the need for life support?

Are there characteristics which mark the various stages in the life cycle of an empire?

To seek to answer these questions in the realm of business, entertainment, communications, politics and a myriad of other areas of life is beyond the scope of this volume. It is, however, the purpose of *When the Empire Strikes Out* to consider the thesis that political empires do have discernible characteristics which mark their life cycle. It is further intended to examine these and compare them with the characteristics of the current culture in order to suggest where we may find ourselves today in the life cycle of the empire we know.

We will pursue this goal with the understanding that "empire," as it will be considered here, means a large state or group of states with international superpower status under a single imperial sovereignty and that the current empire under consideration is the United States of America.

Please join me in this journey of discovery.

PART

2

Sir John Finds a Pattern

A career soldier and statesman with an avid interest in history would certainly appear be a logical individual to analytically discern similarities in the annals of the empires whose exploits fill the historical record.

And so it is.

The late Sir John Glubb identified to an extent unusual among historians a recurring pattern in the life cycle of earth's empires. The pattern is a consistent one which he maintained would enable the people of a culture to identify where they are in their empire's cycle and what the future may hold.

Part Two, then, introduces Sir John, describes the pattern he identified and explores his thesis. It also considers the significant question of the validity of his conclusions.

Chapter Two

Meet Sir John Glubb

*Everything that is occurring around us
has happened again and again before.*

—Sir John Glubb

It was a disciplined but lonely life. He was a ten-year-old boy, the son of an officer in the Royal Engineers who was serving England in Mauritius, an island near Madagascar off the eastern shores of Africa. The Glubb family was there as part of a three-year posting. But young John was in Switzerland, separated from his parents during a year-long stint at school. The year was 1907.

During that era, it was unusual for a youngster of John's age to experience the kind of international travel and schedule disruption that he had already known. Those experiences undoubtedly played a part in opening the lad's mind to the world at large and in piquing his interest in the study of history. It was an interest that would occupy a large role in John Glubb's life as an adult.[1]

In September of 1914, at the age of seventeen, John entered the Royal Military Academy at Woolwich, England. He was commissioned in the Royal Engineers in April of the following year and served throughout the First World War in France and Belgium. John early demonstrated his courage and military bent during that conflict. He was wounded three times and, as a result, received the Military Cross.

Following the war, Sir John volunteered for service in Iraq as a regular officer. Six years later he resigned his commission and accepted an administrative post under the Iraqi government. It was the beginning of a long and distinguished service career in the Middle East. During that time, Sir John became an avid student of history, not only of the Arab peoples but also of the course of empires.

In 1930 Sir John left Iraq and signed a contract to serve the government of Transjordan, forerunner of what is now known as Jordan.

His Career Takes Off

Nine years later, in 1939, just as World War II was beginning, Sir John became commander of the famous Jordan Arab Legion, in reality the Jordanian army. The period of history that followed was full of tension, not only initially in Europe where Hitler was running roughshod over country after country, but also in the Middle East as well.

During Sir John's seventeen-year command, momentous events transpired. In addition to World War II, there was the birth of the nation of Israel in 1948 with resultant battles and tensions. His involvement and leadership during this period was a stabilizing factor for which he was knighted by the Queen. It also contributed to his becoming known as Glubb Pasha, an Arabic term denoting a man of high rank and honor.

An Author and a Lecturer

Following his retirement in 1956, his career entered a new and wider phase. His avid life-long interest in history now found expression in an intensive study of what he saw to be its rhythms and patterns. He began to write extensively and to lecture widely. Eighteen of his books, concentrating chiefly on the Middle East, have been published. Included among them are *The Story of the Arab Legion, Britain and the Arabs, The Empire of the Arabs, The Middle East Crisis, The Course of Empire, The Lost Centuries, Into Battle* and *Arabian Adventures.*[2]

His best-known and most thought-provoking book was published in Scotland in 1976 with several reprintings since. *The Fate of Empires and Search for Survival* became the book form of a series of lectures given by Sir John throughout Britain, the United States and Europe. The material which comprised the bulk of the book first appeared in printed form in *Blackwoods Magazine* during the mid-1970s and occasioned a huge response largely because many readers felt that Sir John was unduly critical of what was left of the British Empire.

Such was not actually the case, for he himself was a product of the military aspect of that once-mighty empire, a true son of proud Britannia. In his comments and conclusions he was simply being faithful to his thesis—that the Age of Decline and Collapse in an empire is marked by indicators which have been consistent throughout history.

At the end of a long and distinguished career, Sir John Glubb passed away in 1987 in his ninetieth year.

Now, in Chapter 3, let's turn our attention away from the historian to a consideration of his conclusions concerning empires.

Endnotes

1. Sir John Glubb's biographical material taken from a brief biography in *The Fate of Empires and Search for Survival*, published in 1981 by William Blackwood and

Sons, Ltd., Edinburgh, Scotland. It is now out of print. See Note 2 for information on how to obtain it.

2. Sir John's papers and writings are archived at Oxford University. For information, contact Sir Marrack I. Goulding, Warden, St. Antony College, Oxford University, University Offices, Wellington Square, Oxford, England OX1 2JD.

Chapter Three

The Fate of Empires

We learn nothing from history
because our studies are too narrow. . . .

—Sir John Glubb

Sir John obviously felt very strongly about it. In his introduction to *The Fate of Empires* he wrote, "My plea is that history should be the history of the human race, not of one small country or period." Later in the same publication, he stated his conviction that "we learn nothing from history because our studies are too narrow—normally limited to our own countries."

Sir John enunciated several reasons why he believed that the broad sweep of human history with its valuable lessons is lost to us. The limitation of much historical work to short periods or a narrow scope such as a particular time period or a single country is the first reason cited.

A second reason for the futility of some historical studies, said Sir John, is the tendency even within the inadequate parameters indicated above to study subjectively rather than objectively. The result, according to him, is that national histories become propaganda, not objective investigations.

The tendency to study short, unconnected but "fashionable" periods while neglecting the intervals between them is a third reason why history's important lessons have not been learned.

To counteract these approaches, Sir John maintained that it is essential to grasp the principle that "history, to be meaningful, must be the history of the human race"—the whole flow of human development. And in seeking to understand the laws which govern the rise and fall of empires it is imperative that the imperial experiments recorded in history *all* be investigated.

While extensive information is not available on every past power, there is much that is known of many empires, certainly of each of the greatest. From such study may be drawn common characteristics which will provide lessons for the current age. In that way the study of history becomes useful.

Practicing What He Preaches

Sir John set himself to do what he urged upon others: he sought to study history as a continuous whole rather than as unrelated segments. And in the matter of empires he looked to see whether instructive similarities were to be found in widely differing imperial powers. He came to the conclusion that indeed such similarities were to be found, "extraordinary similarities," in fact. Regardless of the stage at which it appeared in human history or the ultimate extent of its power, each empire had things in common with other empires.

Seven stages in the rise and fall of empires were thus identified by Sir John. He isolated these ages and finally compiled what he believed to be the common life cycle of empires:

1. The Age of Outburst (or Pioneers)
2. The Age of Conquests
3. The Age of Commerce
4. The Age of Affluence
5. The Age of Intellect
6. The Age of Decadence
7. The Age of Decline and Collapse[1]

It should be noted that in speaking of the life cycle of an empire, Sir John did not suggest that the people of the defunct empire ceased to exist. Rather it is understood that it was the greatness and power of the empire which came to an end though the nation survived nominally. The Arab and the British Empires are two examples. The Arabs and the British continue to exist as peoples and nations but no longer wield empire power.

Regardless of the stage at which it appeared in human history or the ultimate extent of its power, each empire had things in common with other empires.

In the matter of life cycles, it is interesting to note what I believe is Sir John's least convincing argument. He maintains that the length of empire life cycles is similar—an average of 250 years. Listing the duration in years of eleven empires, ranging from a high of over 700 to a low of 208 years, he admitted that the dates he used were largely arbitrary. Further, his suggestion that 250 years represents ten generations is also arbitrary since a wide range of opinion exists on the length of a generation.

Nevertheless, Sir John offers a good deal of historical documentation in support of his thesis of a common life cycle for empires.

Stage One: The Age of Outburst

Concerning this first stage, he observes that "again and again in history we find a small nation, treated as insignificant by its contemporaries, suddenly emerging from its homeland and overrunning large areas
of the world."[2] He offers as examples the amazingly rapid expansion of
several empires—the Macedonian, Arab, Mongol and Spanish—as
typical of empire outburst.

The Macedonian outburst occurred within thirty-six years (359-323
B.C.); the Arab in twenty (A.D. 633-653); the Mongol in forty-five (A.D.
1211-1255); and the Spanish in fifty years (A.D. 1492-1540). Other examples of the sudden outbursts by which empires are born could be
multiplied.

The characteristics which this soldier/historian observes in the Outburst Era of an empire are admirable. Typical was an extraordinary display of energy and courage not only in battle but also in every field of
endeavor. Fearless initiative and bold action characterized the Outburst Period.

Stage Two: The Age of Conquests

The Age of Conquests is a period marked by the continuation of
"amazing initiative, and almost incredible enterprise, courage and har-
dihood."[3] Victories in the march of conquest, though more organized
and disciplined than in the Outburst Age, were won chiefly by "reckless bravery and daring initiative."[4] The initiative of the era found its
outlet also in exploration, pioneering and the push into uncharted areas, with "confidence, optimism and perhaps contempt for the 'decadent' races which have been subjugated."[5]

Sir John writes, "The conquest of vast areas of land and their subjugation to one government automatically acts as a stimulant to commerce."[6] Thus, he says, the third stage of empire followed logically and inevitably overlapped conquest.

Stage Three: The Age of Commerce

Evidence for this may be seen in the fact that vast territories, now separated into as many as several dozen countries, were once under the control of a single imperial authority. Instead of dozens of different laws, policies, customs, currencies and borders which served as a hindrance to commerce, a unified empire—with one set of laws, one official language, one currency and one administration—greatly stimulated commercial ventures.

The Roman Empire is an excellent example of this. Today a number of nations geographically within the boundaries of the ancient empire are attempting to remove, through development of the European Union, national barriers to economic growth, barriers which did not exist under Rome.

Another example of the Age of Commerce is the brutal Mongol Empire with its massacre of entire cities. It nevertheless witnessed caravan trade between China and Europe when the empire extended from Peking to Hungary with the entire territory under one government.

Further indication that far-flung empire commerce existed even in times of slow, premodern transport may be seen in the fact that "objects made in Ireland, Scandinavia and China have been found in the graves or ruins of the Middle East, dating from 1,000 years before Christ."[7] Similar examples of the depth and extent of the empire's influence and power abound.

Stage Four: The Age of Affluence

The rise of commercial prosperity, aided immeasurably by empire conditions, inevitably ushers in the next stage, The Age of Affluence. Sir John observes that the wealth that poured into an empire soon enabled the commercial classes to become immensely rich. Tragically, throughout human history riches have proven to be addictive. The desire is always for more.

Consequently, though proud military traditions still held sway, though the ancient virtues of courage, patriotism and duty were still somewhat in evidence, and though initiative was still shown in the search for profitable enterprises on the frontiers of the empire, in each Age of Affluence the desire to make money gradually gained hold of the populace.

Sir John sees this stage in the life of an empire to be particularly critical, indicating that by the time an empire is fully into the Age of Affluence it may well have passed its "high noon" and is already into the early stages of decline. He offers as examples Rome, during the rule of Augustus; Baghdad, under Harun al-Rashid; the Ottoman Empire in Sulaiman the Magnificent's reign; and Britain in the time of Queen Victoria.[8]

Indicating that each of these periods reveals the same characteristics, Sir John points out that the immense wealth accumulated in the nation dazzled the public. Though vestiges of prior virtues remained, beneath the surface greed for money gradually replaced a sense of duty and public service, a shift from service to selfishness.

A gradually expanding preoccupation with defense also accompanied this burgeoning affluence and greed. Sir John writes, "The empire, immensely rich, is no longer interested in glory or duty, but is only anxious to retain its wealth and luxury. . . . Money being in better supply than courage, subsidies instead of weapons are employed to buy off enemies."[9] This approach is justified by the reasoning that "military readiness, or aggressiveness, is immoral and primitive."[10]

The Great Wall of China, Hadrian's Wall on the Scottish border and the Maginot Line in France are cited as illustrations of the defensiveness that characterizes affluence in an empire. While the question of militarism and force have their pros and cons, Sir John observes that "history seems to indicate that great nations do not normally demilitarize from motives of conscience, but rather because of the weakening of a sense of duty in citizens, and the increase in selfishness, manifested in the desire for wealth and ease."[11]

> **Instead of seeking training which develops patriotism and virtue, parents and students alike pursue the kind of education which will command the highest salaries.**

Education undergoes the same gradual transformation in the Age of Affluence. Instead of seeking training which develops patriotism and virtue, parents and students alike pursue the kind of education which will command the highest salaries. An example of this common attitude is presented in the complaint of the Arab moralist Ghazali (1058-1111), who said that students no longer attended college to acquire learning and virtue, but to obtain those qualifications which would enable them to grow rich.[12]

Stage Five: The Age of Intellect

This next stage of empire life is very closely related to the affluence stage and is unquestionably a product of it.

Since the great wealth of an empire which has become affluent is no longer fully required to supply the necessities or even the luxuries of life, ample funds become available for the pursuit of knowledge. Thus, historically, merchant princes from the commercial realm, seeking fame and honor, founded and/or endowed colleges and universities. Rulers sought to immortalize themselves in the establishment of centers of learning.

An example is that of the Arab Empire in the eleventh century, under the reign of the Seljuk sultan, Malik Shab. Though the empire was already in decline politically, the building of universities and colleges became almost a passion during his rule. Previously, a small number of universities in the major cities had sufficed. Now a university sprang up in almost every town.[13]

Sir John comments on the remarkable regularity with which the Age of Intellect follows wealth in empire after empire, adding that the passion for knowledge is in itself commendable. Some of the positive aspects of this phase include surprising advances in natural science and other fields of endeavor. Negatively, however, he observes that rather inexplicably intellectualism and the loss of a sense of duty or self-sacrifice appear to occur simultaneously in empire life histories.

The Age of Intellect and the final two Ages identified by Sir Glubb tend to overlap one another to some degree. The last two are, in fact, closely related.

Stage Six: The Age of Decadence

Characteristics of the Age of Decadence include growing civil dissensions, the influx of foreigners into the empire's cities, loss of morality, accelerating materialism, increase in the influence of women, the rise of the welfare state, frivolity, pessimism and the weakening of religion.

Sir John offers an example from the Age of Decadence in the Arab Empire, citing the contemporary historians of Baghdad who deeply deplored the degeneracy of their times. Of particular concern to them was the indifference to religion, the increasing materialism and the laxity of sexual morals. The corruption of government officials and their amassing of wealth while in office were also lamented.

There was bitter lament over the extraordinary influence held over young people by popular singers in Baghdad. Their erotic songs, accompanied by the lute, stimulated the increasing use of obscene sexual language and a decline in public morality. The Arab historians, as did the Romans before them, complained also of the increased influence of women in public life, a factor often associated with national decline. Sir John writes:

> When I first read the contemporary descriptions of tenth-century Baghdad, I could scarcely believe my eyes! They might have been taken out of *The Times* today . . . the break-up of the empire, the abandonment of sexual morality, the "pop" singers with their obscene songs, the entry of women into the professions, the introduction of a five-day work week—at a time when declining trade and financial stringency made this unwise. . . .[14]

Another of the frequently repeated phenomena of great empires, according to Sir Glubb, is the influx of foreigners into the capital and major cities. Without suggesting that immigrants are inferior to the older stock, the soldier/historian observes that over a period of time such a cosmopolitan penetration comes to exercise an influence greatly in excess of its numbers. Because each group is different and possesses significant loyalty to their own, they tend to introduce "cracks and divisions" into the empire.

As empires begin to decline in power and wealth, pessimism develops among its peoples and hastens the decline. Strangely enough, frivolity becomes the companion of pessimism, enunciated in the philosophy, "Eat, drink and be merry, for tomorrow we die." Sir John comments, "The resemblance between various declining nations in this respect is truly amazing."[15]

"Decadence is a moral and spiritual disease. It results from too long a period of wealth and power, producing cynicism, decline of religion, pessimism and frivolity."

Perhaps the most dramatic example of this was seen in the Roman Empire during its decadence. Roman mobs demanded free meals and entertainment—"bread and circuses."[16] Sadistic gladiatorial shows, chariot races, theatrical and athletic events became their passion.

"Decadence is a moral and spiritual disease," Sir John wrote. "[It] results from too long a period of wealth and power, producing cynicism, decline of religion, pessimism and frivolity. The citizens of such a nation will no longer make an effort to save themselves, because they are not convinced that anything in life is worth saving."[17]

Stage Seven: The Age of Decline and Collapse

The logical and inevitable outcome of decadence is the actual decline and collapse of an empire. This stage presents a great diversity, depending largely on outside circumstances and other powers which appear at the time of the empire's fall. In some cases, such as the western part of the Roman Empire, barbarians overran it. The Marmaluke Empire of Egypt and Syria fell in a single campaign when conquered by the Ottomans. The Arab Empire simply became fragmented, while the Spanish Empire fell through loss of her colonies but remained as a sovereign nation. Romanov Russia fell to the communist revolution.

Sir John Glubb thus concludes that though the life cycles of great powers are surprisingly uniform, the nature and results of their falls are diverse.

Show Me Your Heroes, I'll Tell You Your Character

It is Sir John's insightful observation that each Age in the history of an empire has its heroes. Understandably, the characteristics of a given stage are reflected in the nature of those who are lionized during it.

The heroes of the Ages of Outburst and Conquest were the soldiers and the pioneers in the first, and, in addition to them, the builders and the explorers in the second. The virtues admired in such heroes were manliness, courage, energy, devotion to duty, patriotism and daring initiative. The training of youth was intentionally rugged and frugal, with the sense of duty to one's nation constantly drummed into the heads of boys and young men.

The successful businessman, the entrepreneur and the astute financial wizard were the heroic personalities of the Age of Commerce and to some degree of the next two stages. In the Age of Affluence, the heroes were the people who could amass tremendous wealth and demonstrate somewhat ostentatiously that they possessed it. Predictably, the academics along with the wealthy were lionized in the Age of Intellect.

And finally, according to Sir John, the heroes of the Ages of Decadence, Decline and Collapse are consistently the same—the athletes, the singers and the actors.

Is he right?

In Chapter 4 we'll consider the validity of Sir John Glubb's observations and perhaps come to a few conclusions of our own.

Endnotes

1. Sir John Glubb, *The Fate of Empires* (Edinburgh: William Blackwood & Sons, Ltd., 1981), 28.

2. Ibid., 4.

3. Ibid., 6.

4. Ibid., 7.

5. Ibid..

6. Ibid., 9.

7. Ibid., 7.

8. Ibid., 9

9. Ibid., 11.

10. Ibid.

11. Ibid.

12. Ibid., 10.

13. Ibid., 12.

14. Ibid., 18.

15. Ibid., 24.

16. Ibid., 23.

17. Ibid., 24.

Chapter Four

A Valid View?

*Caution is . . . in order as we attempt
to trace the course of cultural decay.*

—Charles Colson in *Against the Night*

Caution is, indeed, in order as we explore the validity of Sir John Glubb's historical thesis. It is essential that we pose and seek to carefully answer a most significant question: Do the historical records support Glubb's contention that over the past 4,000 years the life cycles of empires have had remarkable similarities and that the characteristics of an era can provide insight into where current superpowers may be in their own cycles?

We will pursue the answer to that question by examining the evidence. That empires rise and fall is a given, an acknowledged fact which is encapsulated in a poignant incident from Roman times.

The General Wept

Scipio Africanus was a Roman general. He was known for brilliantly rallying Rome's armies from the brink of defeat when the daring strategies of the Carthaginian general, Hannibal, almost spelled an early end to the Roman Empire. Leading a military resurgence that climaxed with the three-year-long Roman siege of Carthage, Hannibal's capital, Scipio finally realized the total conquest and torching of that doomed city in 146 B.C.

The Greek historian, Polybius, reports that as the general stood on a hillside watching Carthage burn, there was no gloating nor even the satisfied smile of a victor. Instead, Scipio Africanus "burst into tears, and stood long, reflecting on the inevitable change which awaits cities, nations, dynasties, *one and all*, as it does every one of us men" (emphasis mine).

Chuck Colson, in commenting on the scene, writes that "Scipio Africanus, the great conqueror and extender of empires, saw the inexorable truth: No matter how mighty it may be, no nation, no empire, no culture is immortal."[1] With such an analysis Sir John Glubb would unquestionably agree.

"No matter how mighty it may be, no nation, no empire, no culture is immortal."—Chuck Colson

---

To search for evidence of Glubb's arbitrary stages in every one of earth's past empires is beyond the scope of this volume even if it were possible. Still, it is feasible to examine several of his stages as representative and thus determine whether the historical record indicates support for or opposition to Sir John's conclusions.

A Valid View?

In particular, it is important for us to explore the rise and fall of the Roman Empire and later inquire if and how Sir John's conclusions apply to America. A comment by Francis Schaeffer in his classic *How Should We Then Live?* explains why Roman history is particularly relevant to us.

> As we try to learn lessons about the primary dilemmas which we now face, by looking at the past and considering its flow, we could begin with the Greeks, or even before the Greeks. We could go back to the three great ancient river cultures: the Euphrates, the Indus and the Nile. However, we will begin with the Romans . . . *because Roman civilization is the direct ancestor of the modern Western world.* From the first conquests of the Roman Empire down to our own day, Roman law and political ideas have had a strong influence on the European scene and the entire Western world. Wherever Western civilization has gone, it has been marked by the Romans (emphasis mine).[2]

Further support both for Sir John's thesis and for focusing on the Roman Empire comes from Dr. James Dobson's book, *Children at Risk*. In a chapter entitled, "Love and Sex," he writes:

> Robbed of sexual standards, society will unravel like a ball of twine. That is the lesson of history. *That is the legacy of Rome* and more than two thousand civilizations that have come and gone on this earth. The family is the basic unit of society on which all human activity rests. If you tamper with the sexual nature of familial relationships, you necessarily threaten the entire superstructure (emphasis mine).[3]

G.K. Chesterton's statement, recorded in *A Chesterton Anthology,* reinforces the concept: "There are commonwealths, plainly to be distinguished here and there in history, which pass from prosperity to squalor, or from glory to insignificance, or from freedom to slavery, not only in silence, but with serenity. The face still smiles while the limbs, literally and loathsomely, are dropping from the body."[4]

Arnold J. Toynbee, author of the classic, *The Study of History*, writes in his introduction on "The Comparability of Societies":

> In fact we maintain that our twenty-one societies should be regarded, hypothetically, as philosophically contemporaneous . . . and equivalent.[5]

> The history of almost every civilization furnishes examples of geographical expansion coinciding with deterioration in quality.[6]

> Disintegration proceeds . . . by an alternation of routs and rallies. This pattern is exemplified in the histories of several extinct societies.[7]

In the concluding chapter of his book, Toynbee argues that ". . . *standardization* is the mark of [the] disintegration [of empires]" (emphasis mine).[8]

And so, with the understanding that all empires do disintegrate, let's look for evidence of the accuracy of Sir John's thesis in the story of past empires, particularly in what is undoubtedly the best known—the Roman Empire. But before we consider Rome in the next chapter, let's take a glance at several other representative past powers.

For Example, Consider . . .

Delving into an intriguing set of history books published over 100 years ago proved to be most instructive for me. The three-volume set, *Seven Great Monarchies of the Ancient Eastern World,* by George Rawlinson, Camden Professor of Ancient History at the University of Oxford, provides interesting insights into empire life cycles.

For example, in his survey of the Median Empire, Rawlinson's book contains numerous statements which support Sir John's thesis. In *Vol-*

ume Two, The Third Monarchy, Media, chapter 6, "Chronology and History," the professor described the period which Glubb terms "The Age of Outburst" using terms such as "the *sudden growth* of Media in power about this period. . ." (emphasis mine). He further noted that "[t]he successes of [King] Cyaxares did but whet his appetite for more power, and stimulate him to attempt further conquests . . . [so that] he *quickly* subdued to himself all Asia above the Halys" (emphasis mine).[9]

He described the ongoing conquests and the growth of wealth (corresponding to Glubb's stages of Conquest and Commerce) with comments like ". . . so soon as Media had proved her strength, first by shaking herself free of the Scythic invaders, and then by conquering Assyria, the tribes [of Asia Minor] accepted her [rule] at once." In terms of its commerce, Rawlinson writes that

> [t]he Median Empire became in extent and fertility of territory equal if not superior to the Assyrian. . . . In fertility its various parts were very unequal; portions were rich and productive, but there were also a large number of barren mountainous regions and some desert. [However,] if we estimate the resources of Media from the data furnished by Herodotus . . . [it is apparent] that the wealth of the Medes exceeded that of Assyria.[10]

Rawlinson also details the decadence and decline that marked the final stages of the empire. His descriptions of the Median Age of Decadence and Decline are quite graphic:

> We are told that the Medes were very luxurious at their banquets. . . . Each guest had his own dishes, and it was a mark of special honor to augment their number. Wine was drunk both at the meal and afterwards, often in undue quantity; and at the close of the feast was apt to be a scene of general turmoil and confusion.[11]

... Towards the latter part of their empire the Medes became a comparatively luxurious people ... adopting an amount of pomp and magnificence to which they were previously strangers, affecting splendor in their dress and apparel, grandeur and rich ornament in their buildings, variety in their banquets. ... [12]

... Astyages, (the final Median ruler) who led a luxurious life, [was] enjoying himself as usual over his wine, surrounded by a crowd of his concubines, eunuchs, singing girls, and dancing girls, [and] called on one of them for a song. [13]

The luxury of the Court corrupted the nobles, who from hardy mountain chieftains, became polite courtiers, magnificent in their apparel, choice in their diet, and averse to all unnecessary exertion. The example of the upper classes [affected] the lower. ... [14]

The summation by Professor Rawlinson is noteworthy. He wrote: "The conquest of a great and luxurious empire by a hardy and simple race, is followed, almost of necessity, by a deterioration in the character of the conquerors, who lose the warlike virtues [of manliness and sacrifice], and too often do not replace them by the virtues of peace." [15]

The summary statement on the Empire of the Medes by Will Durant, in Part 1—*Our Oriental Heritage,* from his monumental ten-volume *The Story of Civilization* series, further tends to confirm Sir John's conclusions. Durant wrote:

Their [the Medes'] degeneration was even more rapid than their rise. Under the [example of King Astyages] the nation forgot its stern morals and stoic ways; wealth had come too suddenly to be wisely used. The upper classes became the slaves of fashion and luxury, the men wore embroidered trousers, the women covered themselves with cosmetics and jewelry, the very horses were often caparisoned in gold. These once simple and pastoral people, who had been glad to be carried in rude wagons with wheels cut roughly out of the trunks of trees, now rode in expensive chariots from feast to feast. ...

When Cyrus, the brilliant young ruler of the Median dependency of Anshan, in Persia, rebelled against [Astyages, effeminate despotic King of the Medes] the Medes themselves welcomed Cyrus' victory. . . . By one engagement Media ceased to be the master of Persia, Persia became the master of Media, and prepared to become master of the whole Near Eastern world.[16]

Here Come the Persians

A careful study of Will Durant's history of the Persian Empire gives further credence to the views of Sir John Glubb. Of Glubb's Age of Outburst period by the Persians, Durant observed:

Cyrus was one of those natural rulers at whose coronation, as Emerson said, all men rejoice. . . . [He quickly] established the Achaemenid Dynasty of "Great Kings," which ruled Persia through the most famous period of history. . . . [H]e organized the soldiery of [conquered] Media and Persia into an invincible army, captured Sardis and Babylon, ended for a thousand years the rule of the Semites in western Asia, and absorbed the former realms of Assyria, Babylonia, Lydia and Asia Minor into the Persian Empire, the largest political organization of pre-Roman antiquity, and one of the best-governed in history. . . . [H]e was the most amiable of conquerors, and founded his empire upon generosity.[17]

Concerning what Sir John would call the Ages of Conquest and Commerce, Durant wrote:

At its greatest extent, under Darius, the Persian Empire included twenty provinces. . . . [from Egypt to Central Asia]. Never before had history recorded so extensive an area brought under one government. . . .

The monuments picture the Persians as erect and vigorous, made hardy by their mountains. . . . The common man was contentedly literate, and gave himself to the culture of the soil. . . . Persia was content to let the nations of the Near East practice the handicrafts while she bought their products with their imperial tribute. She showed more originality in the improvement of communications and transport. Engineers under the instructions of Darius I built great roads uniting the various capitals; one of these highways . . . was fifteen hundred miles long. . . . The largest rivers were crossed by ferries. . . . These roads were built primarily for military and governmental purposes, . . . but they served to stimulate commerce and the exchange of customs, ideas. . . .[18]

"Education becomes . . . an instrument of worldly ambition or of frivolous amusement."—Arnold Toynbee

While Durant does not specifically address Sir John's Age of Intellect in relation to the history of the Persian Empire, another renowned historian, Arnold Toynbee, does describe in general terms the effects of education in ways that confirm Glubb's view:

One stumbling block of education when the process is made available to the masses [is that] education [becomes] either a pearl cast before swine or else a pearl of great price which the finder buys at the cost of all that he has . . . an instrument of worldly ambition or of frivolous amusement.

The possibility of turning education to account as a means of amusement for the masses—and of profit for [enterprising] persons—has only arisen since the introduction of universal education.[19]

Toynbee later illustrates this from the Egyptian Empire:

A Valid View?

The Egyptiac litterati . . . took advantage of [their] knowledge to "bind heavy burdens and grievous to be borne and lay them on men's shoulders" while at the same time the Egyptiac scribes themselves would not move these same burdens "with one of their fingers." This note is struck blatantly in *The Instruction of Duauf,* a work composed during the Egyptiac time of troubles . . . in which a man named Duauf left for his son Pepi [whom he was placing in the School of Books] this parting exhortation: Thou art to set thine heart on books . . . every artisan, every stone-mason, every field-worker, every weaver and fisherman is wearied. Behold, there is no calling that is without [weariness and] a director except [that of] the scribe, and he is the director. . . .[20]

Shifting his focus to the Orient, Toynbee observed: "The Confucian litteratus (an analogue of the Egyptiac 'litteratocracy') used to flaunt his heartless refusal to lift a finger to lighten the load of the toiling millions by allowing his fingernails to grow to lengths which precluded every use of the hand except the manipulation of the scribal brush."[21]

The Persian Age of Decadence and Decline, as Sir John would have termed it, is very clearly detailed by Durant. He wrote that, in contrast to the comparative discipline and character of the Empire's early rulers, "[Persia's] later monarchs delegated most of the cares of government to noble subordinates or imperial eunuchs, and spent their time at love, dice or the chase."[22] His accounts of the decadence are enlightening:

The moral as well as the physical backbone of Persia was broken by Marathon, Salamis and Plataea; the emperors exchanged Mars for Venus, and the empire descended into corruption and apathy. . . . The Persians, like the Medes before them, passed from stoicism to epicureanism in a few generations. Eating became the principal occupation of the aristocracy: these men who had once made it a rule to eat but once a day now interpreted the rule to allow them one meal—prolonged from noon to night; they stocked their larders with a thousand delicacies, and often served entire animals to their guests; they stuffed themselves with rich rare meats, and spent their genius upon new sauces and desserts. Drunkenness became the common vice of every class.[23]

The later monarchs were given to cruelty and dissipation. (The accounts of their almost unspeakable cruelty are best left to the historical records.) In the realm of sexual morality, the "Persians learnt from the Greeks a passion for boys," and licence was the rule of the closing days of empire. Concubines were a luxury of the rich; the aristocracy never went even to war without them. In the later days the king's harem contained from 329 to 360 concubines, for it had become a custom that no woman might share the royal couch twice unless she was overwhelmingly beautiful.[24]

Xerxes was divided by many mistresses, and became for his people an exemplar of sensuality, [while] only the records of Rome after Tiberius could rival in bloodiness the royal annals of Persia.[25]

The final rulers were also obscenely wealthy. When Alexander captured the Persian capitals he found 180,000 talents left in the royal treasuries—some $2,700,000,000—even after Darius III had carried off 8,000 talents in his flight.[26]

"In the realm of sexual morality, licence was the rule of the closing days of empire."—Will Durant

---

As may be observed from the brief documentation presented above, the writings of universally recognized historians present a high degree of confirmation for Sir John's concept of empires having similar stages, each with their particular characteristics.

Beware a Greek Bearing Arms

Greece was another of the major empires whose rise and fall generally fits the pattern presented by Glubb. According to Durant, the early history of what became Greece spanned the period from 9000 B.C. to 1100 B.C., during which various races controlled the area. The end result was a mingling of five cultures: Cretan, Mycenaean, Achaean, Dorian and Oriental. "The mixture of races and ways took centuries to win even a moderate stability, but it contributed to produce the unparalleled variety, flexibility and subtlety of Greek thought and life."[27]

Then, in 336 B.C., after centuries of what were basically civil wars and finally domination by the Persians, Alexander the Great arrived on the scene, and the Greek Age of Outburst dawned. Durant writes:

> On his accession Alexander found himself at the head of a tottering "empire." [He] rose to the situation with a decisive energy that ended all internal opposition, and set the tempo of his career.
>
> He met the first Persian contingent at the river Granicus, and overwhelmed it. . . . At Issus he met the main force of the Persians, 600,000 men, under Darius III. Once more he won by using his cavalry for attack, his infantry for defense. [The conquest of Damascus, Sidon, Tyre, Jerusalem and Gaza was then rapidly accomplished, though Tyre did provide strong resistance.][28]

The Age of Conquest, unbelievably swift, followed immediately:

> The triumphant march of the Greeks was resumed through the Sinai desert into Egypt. . . . Marching back into Asia, Alexander met the vast polyglot army of Darius at Gaugamela, and was dismayed by their multitude. [Nevertheless] his victory was decisive, [whereupon] he received the submission of Babylon . . . reached Susa [taking possession of the city and the $300,000,000 he found in Darius' vaults].

Hardly stopping to rest at Susa, Alexander marched over mountains in the depth of winter to seize Persepolis, and so rapidly did he move that he was in Darius' palace before the Persians could conceal the royal treasury. He [unwisely permitted the sacking and burning of the capital].

The year 327 [B.C.] found him passing over the Himalayas into India, where after crossing the Indus, he defeated King Porus.[29]

Thus in the incredibly short span of thirteen years, from the Outburst in 335 B.C. until the death of Alexander in 323 B.C., the Greeks became Empire. And quite predictably, stages of commerce, affluence and intellect followed until decay finally marked its demise. Of the final Age, Durant observed:

> . . . the pursuit of pleasure [for people now wealthy] consumed the adult life of the upper classes . . . public games had degenerated into professional contests . . . the Greeks, who had once been a nation of athletes, became now a nation of spectators, content to witness rather than do.
>
> Sexual morality was relaxed even beyond the loose standards of the Periclean age. Homosexualism [was] popular . . . the courtesan reigned. . . . Athenian life was portrayed in Menander's plays as a round of triviality, seduction and adultery. Musicians were "handsomely commissioned" and actors, who formed themselves into a union, were "much honored" with [very high incomes] though their morals were low.
>
> The emancipation of women was accompanied by a revolt against maternity, and the limitation of the family became the outstanding phenomenon of the age. . . . Abortion and infanticide [were] common.[30]

Certainly, the broad strokes of history's pen indicate a high degree of similarity between the Grecian Empire and Sir John's pattern of empire.

The Story Is the Same Elsewhere

It is my conclusion that further confirmation, though not presented here, may be found in a study of the history of other empires such as Egypt, Babylonia, Assyria, Lydia and Sparta. Such study must be left to the initiative of the reader, however, since it is clearly beyond the scope of this volume. Consequently, a presentation of the details of such study will not be attempted here—with one exception.

In the next chapter, we will look in some detail at the Roman Empire in view of that empire's enormous and continuing influence on our own Western culture.

Endnotes

1. Charles Colson, *Against the Night* (Ann Arbor, MI: Vine Books, 1989), 16.

2. Francis A. Schaeffer, *How Should We Then Live?* (Old Tappan, NJ: Fleming H. Revell, 1976), 20.

3. James Dobson, *Children at Risk,* as quoted by Billy Graham in *Storm Warning* (Dallas, TX: Word, 1992), 169.

4. Colson, 109.

5. Arnold J. Toynbee, *A Study of History, Abridgement of Volumes I-VI,* by D.C. Somervell (New York & London: Oxford University Press, 1946), 43.

6. Ibid., 191.

7. Ibid., 589.

8. George Rawlinson, *The Seven Great Monarchies of the Ancient Eastern World, Volume II* (New York: A.L. Burt, 1893), 86-89. It is most significant to note that Rawlinson uses as his sources the histories of the Persian contemporary writers, Herodotus and Ctesias.

9. Ibid., 38.

10. Ibid., 42-43.

11. Ibid., 39.

12. Ibid., 111-112.

13. Ibid., 117-118.

14. Ibid., 117.

15. Ibid., 125.

16. Will Durant. *The Story of Civilization, Part I, Our Oriental Heritage* (New York: Simon and Schuster, 1954), 351-352.

17. Ibid., 352.

18. Ibid., 355-358.

19. Toynbee, 292.

20. Ibid., 324-325.

21. Ibid., 325.

22. Durant, 359.

23. Ibid., 381.

24. Ibid., 375.

25. Ibid., 381.

26. Ibid., 383.

27. Will Durant, *The Story of Civilization, Part II, The Life of Greece* (New York: Simon and Schuster, 1939), 64.

28. Ibid., 544.

29. Ibid., 544-546.

30. Ibid., 375-380, 566-568.

Chapter Five

When in Rome . . .

As the Empire ground down, the decadent Romans were given to a thirst for violence and a gratification of the senses . . . especially evident in their rampant sexuality.

—Francis A. Schaeffer in *How Should We Then Live?*

"All roads lead to Rome!" This statement expressing the common attitude in the days of the mighty Roman Empire has come all the way down to us in the twenty-first century. It is but one small example of the impact Rome has had upon the Western world. In the judgment of historian Will Durant, Rome was "the most impressive continuity of government and civilization, [and the greatest empire] in the history of mankind."[1]

But, in addition, Durant was convinced that

the panorama [of the Roman Empire] has a greater meaning for us than through its scope and majesty: it resembles significantly, and sometimes with menacing illumination, the civilization and problems of our day. This is the advantage of studying a civilization in its total scope and life—that one may compare each stage or aspect of its career with a corresponding moment or element of our own cultural trajectory, and be warned or encouraged by the ancient aftermath of a modern phase.[2]

Not Your Average Empire

In comparing Rome with Sir John Glubb's sequence of stages in the life cycle of empires, it soon becomes apparent that the Roman Empire had a life cycle very much like the one Sir John identified, though in some aspects there were exceptions.

Let's check it out.

We begin by reminding ourselves of the order of the stages in an empire's life cycle according to Sir John's thesis. It begins with the Age of Outburst, during which a small nation, considered insignificant by its contemporaries, suddenly emerges from its homeland and overruns large areas of the world. This is followed by the Age of Conquest, when the gains are consolidated and the boundaries of the empire are extended.

The Age of Commerce is next, as business booms under the empire's powerful umbrella and wealth pours into the coffers of the conquerors. Widespread trade leads to and overlaps the Age of Affluence. The abundance of wealth then makes possible the Age of Intellect as institutions of learning are multiplied and education becomes primarily a means to gain wealth or position. The last three mentioned stages overlap to a degree; nonetheless, there is a progression.

Some overlap is also true of the next and seemingly inevitable stage, the Age of Decadence, which in turn is the forerunner of the final Age of Decline and Collapse. We'll look in more detail at the characteristics of Rome's final stages later in the chapter.

You're My Hero!

We also remind ourselves that Sir John postulated that each Age, in addition to its unique characteristics, had its distinct heroes. Soldiers and pioneers were lionized in the Age of Outburst, while in the Age of Conquest, in addition to them, the builders and pioneers were admired. The astute and successful businessmen/entrepreneurs were the heroes of the Age of Commerce, and to a degree of the next two stages as well. The individuals who were able to amass wealth were emulated in the Age of Affluence and, along with the academics, were the greats in the Age of Intellect. According to Sir John, the heroes of the last two Ages—Decline and Collapse—were actors, singers (or musicians) and athletes.

What's the Roman Record?

Historians agree that the Roman Empire had its modest beginnings in 509 B.C., but certainly not entirely in the kind of outburst that Sir John described as being typical of empires. In fact, it's birth was rather unspectacular.

For more than 100 years, Rome, the major city of the Villanovan population of ancient Italy, had been ruled by the Etruscans of whom comparatively little is known. Then in 509 B.C., as tradition has it, Rome suddenly overthrew Tarquin, the Etruscan king, became a republic and began her long struggle to dominate Italy and the world.

The initial uprising was a backlash against the rape of Lucretia, the beautiful and virtuous wife of the Roman general Lucius Collatinus, by Sextus Targuinius, son of Tarquin Superbus (meaning "the Proud"). Lucretia told her father and her husband about the rape, made them swear vengeance and then stabbed herself to death. Her cousin, Lucius Junius Brutus, agitated against the Tarquins, raised a people's army and drove out the Etruscans. Thus Rome was freed from Etruscan ascendancy and came under the rule of an aristocracy that lasted until Caesar [44 B.C.].[3]

In that sense the Empire began with an outburst, but the initial action was not followed immediately by the rapid acquisition of territory. Rather, the Age-of-Conquest march toward world domination was a comparatively long one with its share of setbacks.

First, the three Samnite Wars (thirty-seven years of struggle over a fifty-three-year period); second, the three Punic Wars (forty-five years of battle in a 118-year period); and third, the three Macedonian Wars (fifteen years out of a forty-six-year period). During the Second Punic War, the daring Carthaginian general, Hannibal, with his elephant-equipped army actually threatened Rome itself, inflicting several major defeats upon the Roman legions. Nevertheless, the Empire steadily grew through conquest, sporadic as it may have seemed.

- By 283 B.C. most of Greek Italy was occupied.
- Sicily became a Roman province in 241 B.C. during the First Punic War; Sardinia and Corsica in 238 B.C.
- Gaul was conquered in 222 B.C.
- Syracuse was conquered in 212 B.C., and Spain in 201 B.C.
- The Carthaginians and the Greeks were defeated in 146 B.C.

Now, the rule of Rome encompassed Italy, all of North Africa and Greece.

During the 210 years between 139 B.C. and A.D. 71 three wars were fought during which Egypt was annexed to the Empire (A.D. 30), as were parts of Germany and Britain (A.D. 55-75) Further territorial gains followed sporadically in the next several hundred years. Thus the Conquest stage of the Roman Empire encompassed 700 years, reaching its zenith in A.D. 300 during the reign of Diocletian.[4]

How Is Sir John Doing So Far?

Reflecting at this point on the history of the Roman Empire and a comparison of it with Sir John's thesis of uniform stages in empire life cycles, we must give the soldier/historian mixed grades.

Unquestionably Rome had an Age of Outburst—of sorts. Then, as we have just rehearsed, there can be no doubt concerning her Age of Conquest. In this, Sir John is right. However, the kind of Outburst and its relationship in time to the Conquest stage are rather different than what Sir John would suggest as the pattern in empires. The longevity of Rome's rule is also hundreds of years above the average empire life span indicated by Glubb (though Sir John himself admitted that the length of the life span of empires was an average). Basically, however, Rome's early history does support Sir John's thesis.

Let's now go beyond the Age of Conquest and consider the remainder of Glubb's Ages in relation to Rome.

Such Wealth, Such Splendor, Such Power

The extent and power of the Empire meant that fabulous wealth flowed into her coffers and into the hands of numerous individuals. Durant writes:

> [Rome's] boundaries had been extended beyond the Danube, into Scotland and the Sahara, into the Caucasus and Russia, and to the gates of Parthia. She had accomplished for that confusion of people and faiths a unity, not of language or culture, but of economy and law. She had woven it into a majestic commonwealth, within which the exchange of goods moved in unprecedented plenty and freedom; . . . all the world looked to her as the center of the universe, the omnipotent and eternal city. Never had there been such wealth, such splendor or such power. . . . [No one] carries through any business without the in-

tervention of a Roman citizen; not a penny changes hands without passing through the ledgers of a Roman.[5]

Men became millionaires or more through acquisition, speculation, political favor and intrigue. Fabulous fortunes were made, such as that of Crassus, whose personal treasury grew to 170,000,000 sesterces [$25,500,000—the Bill Gates of the era?]. Lucius Lucullus, a honored general, built one palace with spacious halls, loggias, libraries and gardens. He also owned another estate that stretched for miles, bought a third villa for 10,000,000 sesterces [$1,500,000] and turned an entire island into his summer resort. One of his dining rooms was reserved primarily for feasts costing [$30,000] or more.[6]

Nearly everybody in Rome worshiped money with mad pursuit . . . [so that] a century later the satirist Juvenal sarcastically [spoke of] "the most holy wealth." One senator, Gnaeus Lentulus, had [$5,634,000], but with this exception the greatest fortunes in Rome were those of businessmen.[7]

One such was the merchant Trimalchio, whose estates were so vast that a daily gazette had to be written to keep him abreast of his earnings. The description of one single banquet he gave covered forty pages.[8]

The affluence which Rome's vast wealth produced almost beggars description. Hinted at in the quotes above, it can scarcely be imagined. A passage in *Roman Antiquities* summarizes it well:

The ancient Romans lived on the simplest fare . . . but when riches were introduced . . . luxury seized all classes. The pleasures of the table became the chief object of attention. Everything was ransacked to gratify the appetite.[9]

Equipped with such [wealth] the Roman patriciate and upper middle class passed with impressive speed from stoic simplicity to reckless luxury. Houses became larger . . . furniture grew lavish. . . . Great sums were paid for Babylonian rugs, for couches inlaid with ivory, silver or gold; precious stones and metals shone on tables and chairs, on the bodies of women, on the harness[es] of horses. As physical exertion diminished and wealth expanded, the old simple diet gave way to long and heavy meals of meat, game, exotic foods, delicacies and condiments. Drinking increased; goblets had to be large and preferably of gold; wine was less diluted, sometimes not at all.[10]

"The pleasures of the table became the chief object of attention. Everything was ransacked to gratify the appetite."—Alexander Adam

Good Old School Days

An aspect of these somewhat overlapping Ages of Commerce and Affluence was the development of the Age of Intellect which also overlapped but nevertheless came in progression. Durant writes of this period that "private libraries were now numerous . . . Asinius Pollio made his great collection the first public library in Rome. . . . Stimulated by these facilities, Roman literature and scholarship began to equal the industry of the Alexandrians."[11] He further notes:

The Roman equivalent of our college and university education was provided in the schools of the rhetors. The Empire bristled with rhetoricians. . . . Petronius complained that education unfitted youth for the problems of maturity. . . . By Vespasian's time the schools of rhetoric had so grown in number and influence that the wily Emperor thought it advisable to bring the more important ones in the capital under government control. . . . By the reign of Hadrian governmental financing of secondary schools had been adopted in many municipalities throughout the Empire. . . . Education reached its height while superstition grew, morals declined and literature decayed.[12]

> Rome did not invent education, but she developed it on a scale un-
> known before, gave it state support and formed the curriculum. . . .[13]

Without question, though perhaps not to the same extent as other empires, Rome's Age of Intellect tends to confirm further Sir John's pattern.

It's All Downhill from Here

The support of history for the concept of the Ages of Decadence and Decay and Collapse in an empire is enormous when one considers the Roman Empire. Historian after historian describes, often in detail, this aspect. Could it be that because, in addition to the facts, the subject seems to hold morbid appeal?

"After a diligent inquiry," Gibbon, in *The Decline and Fall of the Roman Empire,* writes of "four principle causes of the ruin of Rome: (1)The injuries of time and nature, (2) The attacks of the Barbarians, (3) The use and abuse of the materials, and (4) The domestic quarrels of the Romans. Without question the last two mentioned causes, upon investigation, are found to be descriptions of serious moral decline."[14]

Further, in his *In a Study of History*, Toynbee summarizes this stage with comments such as "abandon [was the] substitute for creativity . . . a sense of drift, the sense of sin and the sense of promiscuity [became] substitutes for the joy that accompanies growth . . . vulgarity and barbarism [was everywhere] in art and life. . . ."[15]

The History of Nations, edited by Henry Cabot Lodge, states,

> Socially, no less than politically or financially, the period is one of dec-
> adence, and is marked by growing extravagance and frivolity. Enjoy-
> ment lost all freshness and spontaneity, and became laborious. Animal
> hunts and gladiatorial games became the chief feature in the public fes-
> tivals.

Houses and gardens reached fabulous prices, gambling and extravagance in dress were fashionable foibles, but the favorite mode of expenditure was the luxuries on the table . . . guests were expected
merely to taste of the multitude of dishes served up to them.[16]

A History of Private Life: From Pagan Rome to Byzantium reinforces these descriptions of a decadent, desensitized lifestyle:

> Rather than build dams or docks, cities and their benefactors ruined
> themselves building aqueducts [to supply water to the public baths],
> theaters, gigantic stadiums and amphitheaters. . . . "The theater is las-
> civiousness, the Circus, suspense, and the arena, cruelty." . . . Gladia-
> tor fights were not mere fencing matches with actual risks. The whole
> point was to witness the death of one of the combatants, or better still,
> the decision whether to slit the throat or spare the life of a fallen gladia-
> tor who, exhausted and frightened for his life, was reduced to begging
> for quarter.[17]

Will Durant's classic, *Caesar and Christ*, is literally filled with
graphic and often disturbing accounts of the astonishingly rapid decadence of the once-disciplined Romans as the Ages of Commerce and
Affluence ran their course. A sampling follows:

> Prostitution flourished. Homosexualism was stimulated by contact
> with Greece and Asia: many rich men paid a talent [$3,600] for a male
> favorite; Cato complained that a pretty boy cost more than a farm.[18]
>
> The Triumvir Mark Antony . . . scandalized even Caesar by keeping
> a harem of both sexes in Rome, and traveling with a Greek courtesan in
> his litter. . . . Antony surrendered to such sensuality that his subjects
> lost respect for his authority. He surrounded himself with dancers, mu-
> sicians, courtesans, and roisterers, and took wives and concubines
> whenever a fair woman struck his fancy. . . . [His affair with Cleopatra
> is well-known.][19]

The wretched Emperor Caligula lived "in habitual incest with all his sisters." To other desired women he sent letters of divorce in their husband's names, and invited them to his embraces; there was scarcely one woman of rank he did not approach. Amid these and some homosexual amours he found time for four marriages. . . . In his imperial frolic government was an aside . . . left to "inferior minds." He took his baths not in water, but in perfumes; on one banquet he spent [$150,000—converted from sesterces]. He built great pleasure barges with colonnades, banquet halls, baths, gardens, fruit trees, and gem-set sterns. To raise funds for his saturnalia, Caligula levied taxes upon everything, including the earnings of prostitutes. He had rich men accused of treason and condemned to death as an aid to the Treasury. He personally auctioned off gladiators and slaves. Those who fell into his disfavor were speedily murdered.[20]

Nero was as bad, or worse. His instincts "inclined him to excessive eating, exotic desires, extravagant banquets where the flowers alone cost [$500,000]." An uninhibited satyr, Nero divorced one wife, murdered his own mother, frequented brothels, killed a pregnant second wife, then in regret found a youth who closely resembled her, had him emasculated, married him and "used him in every way like a woman." He launched a horrible wave of violent persecution against Christians, whom he publicly blamed for the fire that razed two-thirds of Rome.[21]

The Romans, like the Greeks, readily condoned the resort of men to prostitutes. The profession was legalized . . . some women enrolled as prostitutes to avoid the legal penalties of detected adultery . . . these "ladies of easy persuasion" could be met everywhere—under the porticoes, at the circus, in the theater, "as numerous as stars in the sky."

Male prostitutes were also available . . . homosexualism flourished . . . as did pederasty. Erotic poetry of indifferent worth and gender circulated freely among sophisticated youth and immature adults. "Seldom do marriages last until death." [22]

Juvenal, the satirist, is disgusted above all by sexual excesses and perversions: by the roue who on marrying finds that his lechery has left him impotent; by the dandies whose manners, perfumes and desires make them indistinguishable from women.[23]

We are assured that the Emperor Commodus drank and gambled, wasted public funds, kept a harem of 300 women and 300 boys, and liked to vary his sex occasionally. . . . Tales of his unbelievable cruelty are transmitted to us. . . . Commodus yielded the reins of government to [his praetorian prefect] and abandoned himself to sexual dissipation.[24]

The History of Nations makes this summary:

Perhaps the most significant mark of the corruption of the age is the frequency of divorce and the general aversion to marriage. There were exceptions, especially among the rural towns, but immorality was the rule.

[There were] two predominant classes in the state . . . the mass of beggars and the [incredibly wealthy], with enormous fortunes possessed by individuals. The result was . . . economic and moral disintegration. The Roman plebeian became a lazy mendicant, fonder of gazing at the theater than of working. The gladiatorial games flourished as never before . . . unbounded and tasteless luxury everywhere prevailed: huge sums were lavished on politics and on the theater to the corruption of both. [25]

"Perhaps the most significant mark
of the corruption of the age [was]
the frequency of divorce and the general
aversion to marriage."—Henry Cabot Lodge

Concerning the final stage in an empire life cycle, Bill Gothard in *Be Alert to Spiritual Danger*, writes:

Rome conquered Greece and became a great world power. However, the Romans hired the Greeks to teach their children. The national sin of Greece, for which God destroyed it, was sodomy. The sin of sodomy is the final stage of moral decay in a society. By its very nature it cannot be contained or controlled once it is given public acceptance. It constantly preys upon new victims. When God-given sexual desires are once fulfilled in a perverted way, there is a binding association with perversion. A cycle of destruction begins as new passions and perversions are sought to replace burned-out lusts. Soon the high moral standards which made Rome a great nation and military power were corrupted and the empire crumbled.[26]

Charles Colson, in *Against the Night*, summarizes Rome's Ages of Decadence, Decline and Collapse:

Rome was already weakened by internal political power struggles among its leaders and indolence among its citizens. Thousands had lived on the dole for years, subsisting complacently on public assistance and free public amusements such as gladiator combat and chariot races. All this combined with the assimilation of barbarians inside the empire's borders gradually diluted the traditional Roman character that had put such a premium on organization, discipline and obedience.

With the loss of these attributes, restraints on the passions fell away. Rome's leaders competed in ever-escalating excesses of decadence— buying, bedding and killing both humans and animals with unrestrained cruelty and concupiscence. Following their leaders, the citizens soon sank into cheaper versions of the same decadence, sating themselves on the blood-letting at the Colosseum, where men and beasts were forced to fight to the death.[27]

More Signs That the End Is Near

Sir John Glubb observed that the final stage of empire is marked by several characteristics: defensiveness, increased immigration, a welfare state and an increasingly dominant role for women. Certainly Rome exhibited these, as the various historians reveal.

Historian Frank Colby, in *Outlines of General History,* describes the defensiveness of the final stages:

> It is now sufficient to state merely that this reverse [the disastrous defeat and destruction of the Roman army of Varus by barbarians] changed the policy of Rome; henceforth she contented herself with a policy of self-defense, maintaining the line of the frontier, but not as a rule seeking to extend her power beyond it to the north.[28]

Durant and Colson both comment on the increased immigration which characterized the Decline. Durant writes,

> If Rome had not engulfed so many men of alien blood in so brief a time [she might have prolonged her days]. . . .[29]

> If we add to the Greeks, the Syrians, the Egyptians, and the Jews some Numidians, Nubians, and Ethiopians from Africa; a few Arabs, Parthians, Cappadocians, Armenians, Phrygians, and Bithynians from Asia; powerful "barbarians" from Dalmatia, Thrace, Dacia, and Germany; mustachioed nobles from Gaul, poets and peasants from Spain, and "tattooed savages from Britain"—we get a picture of a very heterogeneous Rome. . . . Daily friction with groups of different customs [wore] away still more of their custom-made morality.[30]

In the matter of welfare, Durant describes how ". . . by donatives, public works and doles, the rulers deliberately based their powers upon the favor of the army, the proletariat, and the peasantry,"[31] but says that ". . . the dole weakened the poor."[32]

Concerning the increasing dominance of women in the empire's Age of Decline, *The History of Nations* contains this comment: "Women were not content with their own domain. They invaded the realm of politics, attended political conferences, and took their part in all the coterie intrigues of the time."[33]

Durant records that "even in government the role of women grew. [One writer] cried out that 'all other men rule over women; but we Romans, who rule all men, are ruled by our women.' "[34]

> The "emancipation" of women was as complete then as now, barring the formalities of the franchise and the letter of dead laws. It, as in our time, meant industrialization. Some women worked in shops or factories, especially in the textile trades; some became lawyers and doctors; some became politically powerful; the wives of provincial governors reviewed and addressed troops. Conservatives moaned and gloated over the apparent fulfillment of Cato's warning that if women achieved equality they would turn it into mastery. . . . Juvenal was horrified to find women actresses, athletes, gladiators, poets. Martial describes them as fighting wild beasts, even lions, in the arena. . . . It was a colorful, multisexual society . . . [in which] women filled the villas and resorts with their laughter, their proud beauty, their amorous audacities and political intrigue.[35]

The Pattern Is Confirmed

Pausing at this point to compare Sir John's profile of empire life cycles with what the historical records reveal about the Roman Empire leads us to acknowledge that his profile fits quite well.

Though not all of the Ages unfolded in Rome just as Sir John described them, nonetheless the pattern is there. Particularly is this true of the final stages, with their marks of decadence, their unique characteristics and their unworthy heroes.

Ah! those heroes. A brief consideration of who they were in Rome as the Empire died is in order.

An Heroic Lot

According to Sir John's thesis, the heroes of the final Age of an empire—the Age of Decline and Collapse—are the actors, the singers (or musicians) and the athletes. How was it in Rome? Let's allow the historians to answer.

From *Roman Antiquities* we learn that actors were both popular and prominent:

> The most famous and celebrated pantomime was Pylades, the great favorite of the public. . . . What Cicero says, in two of his orations in honor of the comedian Roscius, proves that the Roman people knew "how to recognize merit. . . . In the tragedy of Brutus, Cicero was proclaimed savior of the Commonwealth, and a thousand voices repeated the homage."[36]

"Stars dominated the stage and made huge fortunes."—Will Durant

In Durant's *Caesar and Christ* are descriptions of the balladeer Ovid:

> His racy couplets about [a pretty courtesan, Corinna] had no trouble finding a publisher; under the title of *Amores* they were soon on the lips and lyres of all youthful Rome.
>
> He wrote a lost play, *Medea*, which was well received, but for the most part he preferred "the slothful shade of Venus," and was content to be the "well-known singer of his worthless ways."
>
> Buoyant with success, Ovid issued a manual of seduction, and another treatise on curing love. These little volumes sold so well that Ovid soared to heights of insolent fame. He wrote, "So long as I am

celebrated all the world over, it matters not to me what one or two pettifoggers say about me. . . ."[37]

Stars dominated the stage and made huge fortunes. Aesopus the tragedian, after a life of assiduous extravagance, nevertheless left 20,000,000 sesterces. Roscius, the comic actor, made 500,000 sesterces a year and became so rich that for several seasons he acted without pay—[a gesture] that made this ex-slave the lion of aristocratic gatherings.

Rome welcomed the new art [of pantomime], thrilled to the grace and skill of the actors. . . . Audiences divided into frantic cliques and claques in support of rival favorite [actors]; women of high station fell in love with the actors, and pursued them with gifts and embraces. . . .

The Romans loved music only less than power, money, women and blood. Professional musicians went on extended concert tours throughout the Empire, earning plaudits, fees, public monuments, and infatuations; some, says Juvenal, sold their love for an added honorarium. Women fought for the plectra with which famous players had touched the strings, and offered sacrifices at the altars for the victory of their musical favorites in the Neroian and Capitoline games.[38]

The gladiatorial games were some of the most exciting events of the Roman year, most of which took place in celebration of religious festivals . . . graffiti proclaimed the valor of famous gladiators like Celadus—"the maiden's sigh"—or breathed devotion to a favorite actor.

Still more exciting were the chariot races at the Circus Maximus. . . . At home, in school, in lectures, in the forums, half the talk was about favorite jockeys and charioteers; their pictures were everywhere, their victories were announced in the Acta Diurna; some of them made great fortunes, some had statues raised to them in public squares. On the appointed day, 180,000 men and women moved in festive colors to the enormous hippodrome. Enthusiasm rose to a mania. As the horses or chariots clattered to the final post of a race the hypnotized audience rose like a swelling sea, gesticulated, waved handkerchiefs, shouted and prayed, groaned and cursed, or exulted in almost supernatural ec-

stasy. The applause that greeted the winner could be heard far beyond
the limits of the city.[39]

The historians make it very clear: Rome's heroes in her Age of Decline and Collapse were indeed the actors, the singers and the athletes.
Sir John was right.

So What's the Conclusion?

I must be completely candid at this point.

I have not personally examined, in detail, every one of earth's past empires, not even every major one, in an effort to check out the validity of Sir
John Glubb's thesis. Such an effort would be the work of a lifetime!

However, I have carefully researched enough of the history of mankind's empires, primarily in Will Durant's massive ten-volume *The Story
of Civilization*, as well as other records, to conclude to my own satisfac-
tion that Sir John was basically correct in his conclusion that there is a
similarity in the life cycle of empires common enough to be called a pattern.

And I agree with Sir John's statement that the value of investigating
the imperial experiments recorded in history is to "endeavor to deduce
from them any lessons which may seem applicable to them all."[40]

D.M. Low, in the introduction to his abridgement of Gibbon's *Decline and Fall of the Roman Empire*, makes a similar observation. He
writes, "Today those who feel they are living in a crumbling civilization may find much to compare in the story of the Roman Empire's decline."[41] And Will Durant's comment is also significant. He observes
that the study of history is of value because "one may compare each
stage or aspect of [an empire's] career with a corresponding moment or
event of our own cultural trajectory and be warned. . . ."[42]

That's the next step for us. In Part Three we will look at North America's culture in the light of history to get an idea of where we may stand in the ongoing saga of men and of nations.

Endnotes

1. Will Durant, *The Story of Civilization, Part III, Caesar and Christ* (New York: Simon and Schuster, 1944), 672.

2. Ibid., viii.

3. James Trager, *The People's Chronology, A Year by Year Record of Human Events from Pre-History to the Present* (New York: Henry Holt and Company, 1992), 14, and Durant, 15, 16.

4. Durant, *Chronological Tables,* 20, 110, 210, 452.

5. Ibid., 448, 130.

6. Ibid., 131-132.

7. Ibid., 332.

8. Ibid., 295.

9. Alexander Adam, *Roman Antiquities* (New York: Collins, Keese and Company, 1836), 302-303.

10. Durant, 88.

11. Ibid., 159.

12. Ibid., 367-369.

13. Ibid., 671.

14. Edward Gibbon, as cited by Larry Poland in *How to Prepare for the Coming Persecution* (San Bernadino, CA: Here's Life Publishers, 1990), 59.

15. Arnold J. Toynbee. *A Study of History, Abridgement of Volumes I-IV* (New York, London: Oxford University Press, 1947), 585-587.

16. Henry Cabot Lodge, editor-in-chief, *The History of Nations, Volume III, Rome* (New York: P.F. Collier and Son, 1907), 248.

17. Philippe Aries and Georges Duby, general editors, *A History of Private Life: From Pagan Rome to Byzantium* (Cambridge, MA, London, UK: Belknap Press of Harvard University Press, 1897), 201.

18. Durant, 89.

19. Ibid., 203-204.

20. Ibid., 265-269.

21. Ibid., 275-278.

22. Ibid., 368-370.

23. Ibid., 438.

24. Ibid., 447.

25. Lodge, 382-383.

26. Bill Gothard, *Be Alert to Spiritual Danger* (Oak Brook, IL: Institute in Basic Youth Conflicts, 1979), 11, 16.

27. Charles Colson, *Against the Night* (Ann Arbor, MI: Servant Publications, 1989), 56.

28. Frank Colby, *Outlines of General History* (New York: American Book Company, 1899), 173.

29. Durant, 366.

30. Ibid., 364-365.

31. Ibid., 633.

32. Ibid., 666.

33. Lodge, 384.

34. Durant, 89.

35. Ibid., 370.

36. Adam, 236-241.

37. Durant, 254-255.

38. Ibid., 378-384.

39. Ibid., 381-383, 459.

40. Sir John Glubb, *The Fate of Empires* (Edinburgh: William Blackwood & Sons, Ltd., 1981), 5.

41. Gibbon, xiv.

42. Durant, viii.

PART

3

Will History Repeat Itself?
(Maybe)

Having been introduced to Sir John Glubb and his thesis that all empires have a similar life cycle, and having checked his theory against the historical record—with the conclusion that it is valid—the time has come to take a look at our own culture.

Are we witnessing in the current empire a repetition of the pattern of past imperial powers?

Will history actually repeat itself, or does the fact that we are in the age of an incredible advance in knowledge and technological skill make a difference?

Will our culture be the exception?

Let's explore these questions.

Chapter Six

Take, for Example, the United States

Of ourselves the Roman story is told.

— Will Durant in *Caesar and Christ*

As I examine parallels between American society and other great empires in history, I am often stunned by the way our civilization mirrors the fallen giants of the past.

—Jim Nelson Black, author of
When Nations Die: Ten Warning Signs of a Culture in Crisis

There's no argument about it: Our world has only one superpower left. With the collapse of the Soviet Union, the "evil empire" that for decades craved world supremacy, the United States stands alone as the world's most powerful entity militarily, economically and politically. She is "empire" today, though perhaps not exactly in the sense of past powers.

Sir John Glubb's comment about the United States, written decades ago, is insightful: "The United States arose suddenly as a new nation, and its period of pioneering was spent in the conquest of a vast continent, not an ancient empire. Yet the subsequent life history of the United States has followed the standard pattern . . . the periods of the pioneers, of commerce, of affluence, of intellectualism and of decadence."[1]

"[T]he subsequent life history of the United States has followed the standard pattern. . . ."—Sir John Glubb

---

If Sir John thought that the United States had arrived at the stage of decadence back in the 1970s, one wonders what his assessment would be now! Has the only empire of the new millennium moved on to its final stage—Decline?

Here's the Approach

As we explore this question, we will confine ourselves primarily to a consideration of the characteristics of the last stage in Sir John's paradigm of empires, setting them against the current scene in America. In so doing, we will bypass an undertaking to document the fact that the first stages of empire have, indeed, basically been enacted in the history of the U.S. While this could certainly be done, and will be alluded to occasionally, it is not our focus at this point.

Instead, we will focus primarily on five key characteristics of the age as they relate to current American culture: defensiveness, immigration, the welfare state, the dominance of women and the heroes of the age, followed by the several aspects of the climate in which these characteristics are found. These characteristics are evident against the backdrop of an almost unbelievable affluence even in times of potential recession. Thus, before looking at the characteristics themselves, a consideration of America's affluence is in order.

Affluent America

In September 1999, *Forbes* magazine announced in its annual review of the 400 wealthiest U.S. citizens that for the first time in history the richest Americans had amassed a total net worth of $1 trillion, a figure greater than the gross domestic product of China.

A survey of people with a net worth of $1 to $4 million finds that most do not feel wealthy and would require a worth of $5 million or more in order to do so.[2] Meanwhile the number of National Football League players earning $1 million or more per season rose from less than fifty in 1990 to over 500 by the end of the decade.[3]

The total number of billionaires on the annual list increased by seventy-nine to 258, making 1999 the first time billionaires made up more than half of the list. In order to qualify for the 1999 *Forbes* 400 list, the minimum net worth was $625 million, up from $500 million the year before.[4] There are currently about 8 million millionaires in the U.S. with the projection of 50 million by 2020.[5]

Microsoft chairman, Bill Gates, topped the list with a net worth at that time of $85 billion. Microsoft co-founder, Paul Allen, in second place with $40 billion, recently teamed up with Eurythmics star, Dave Stewart, to launch a New Age TV network. Allen, retired from Microsoft since 1982, stages parties on a grand scale, reminiscent of Rome's glory days. For one such party he chartered a luxurious cruise ship and flew 400 guests to join him for four days in Alaska at an estimated cost of $15 million.[6]

A report in TIME magazine puts individual wealth in America into some degree of perspective. The combined wealth of the three richest men in the U.S.—Bill Gates, Paul Allen and Warren Buffet—exceeds by $20 billion the *combined* Gross National Product of the forty-three poorest nations in the world in which more than 600 million people live![7]

Examples of the affluence of the culture could be multiplied ad nauseam:[*]

- the entertainer Madonna buys a house in London for $15 million[8]
- $1,267,500 is paid for one of Marilyn Monroe's dresses (termed "the bargain of the century" by the purchaser who was "prepared to go much higher"), $268,800 for her traveling case, $145,600 for her temporary driver's license[9]
- a diamond ring-necklace-earrings set goes for almost $3.5 million[10]
- an American multimillionaire successfully concludes a two-year hunt at a cost of $1.1 million by bagging a bighorn sheep in Canada's Jasper National Park[11]
- actor Rowan Atkinson, comedy show arch bumbler "Mr. Bean," bangs up his $1.3 million sports car in a collision.[12]
- the Neiman Marcus group sells all 200 of its limited edition 2000 Ford Thunderbirds (at $42,000 each) in less than two hours[13]
- a Van Gogh painting is purchased for $82.5 million[14]

---

[*] Because fresh examples of America's affluence seem to occur daily, it is impossible to be current with such in a book format. The reader is encouraged to personally spot affluence indicators as they are presented by the media.

- the owner of priceline.com, Richard Braddock, and his wife Susan, rent a $27 million, 23,000-square-foot Aspen, Colorado, home just for the Christmas holidays at a cost of $388,625[15]
- *Newsweek* does a feature story on "Performance Cuisine" which advises, "Forget the food. In the Age of Affluence, it's all about atmosphere: Picassos, [200-foot] shimmering waterfalls and a [four-story] glass-enclosed tower of 10,000 of the best wines served by a leotard-clad 'wine angel' who dons a harness and is hoisted up to fetch the bottle ordered." That, and an $80 tasting menu.[16]
- Madonna signs a $46 million deal with Microsoft to broadcast one of her London concerts on the Internet.[17]
- fifty-six-year-old actor Michael Douglas and thirty-one-year-old actress Catherine Zeta-Jones, who gave birth to the couple's son three months before, exchange vows in a $2 million wedding in New York's Plaza Hotel. Dubbed the "Wedding of the Millennium," the event attracted media from as far away as Japan and Argentina. *OK!* magazine reportedly paid $2.2 million for exclusive rights to cover the ceremony.[18]

Add affluence indicators like these: In Las Vegas, gambling capital of the nation, where new mega-resorts must be continually developed to remain competitive, you'll find resorts like Paris Las Vegas, a twenty-four-acre property which re-creates famous Parisian landmarks, including a fifty-story replica of the Eiffel Tower, a two-thirds replica of the Arc de Triomphe and much more.

Just down the street is the New York, New York Hotel & Casino where there's a 150-foot replica of the Statue of Liberty and twelve skyscrapers from the New York skyline re-created in the facade—the tallest being a 529-foot, forty-seven-story Empire State Building.[19]

Or consider the proliferation of trendy and expensive spas, the "hippest" of which, Bliss in New York City, recently sold a seventy-percent share for $30 million.[20]

The indications of outrageous expressions of affluence keep on appearing. A news item in *The Report* describing the growing industry of pet care details some of the services offered: "individual theme cottages complete with TV/VCR; temperature-controlled limousine pickup/drop off including background music in a stress-free atmosphere; Internet viewing; massage, music, sightseeing, Sparkletts bottled water, biscuits, doggy cologne; supervised play with a trained staff; 24-hour human companionship, cuddle time and more." All for only $20 to $30 a day! Pet lovers complain about a shortage of dog blood donors and beds in dog hospitals. One owner spent over $13,000 having an oncologist, cardiologist and several "holistic" vets provide chemotherapy, radiation and acupuncture treatment for his ten-year-old dog's lymphoma.[21]

Affluent golfers are beginning to show up on the links—at which $100,000 memberships are common—in "loaded" $25,000 golf carts rebuilt to look like BMWs, Cadillacs and Ferraris.[22]

According to a *WORLD* magazine report,

Americans are enjoying the fruit . . . of rising incomes as they go on one of history's biggest consumption binges. . . . Luxury car sales jumped seven percent in the first quarter of the year [2000], while sales of personal and corporate jets reached a 15-year high. Consumers are on a spending roll, and not just for the little luxury items. Homes are a major part of the surge.[23]

On a much smaller, but still affluent scale, Catholics can now confess in a "luxury state-of-the-art confessional" valued at $10,000. And the battle for custody of Caleigh, the four-year-old daughter of Revlon billionaire Ron Perelman and Patricia Duff, featured demands from

Patricia for child support of $4,400 a day and $1.13 million a year in alimony to raise the tot. "Why so much? How about a $19,500 desk for starters?" Appropriately, perhaps, in a recent "first," Perelman became the model for a grossly flamboyant billionaire character in a daily comic strip.[24]

Other indicators of affluence: A floor price of $2.5 million for the penthouse loft of the late John Kennedy, Jr., peanuts compared to the $9.5 million paid for the New York co-op owned by his late mother, Jacqueline Onassis.[25]

The popularity of the TV show, "Who Wants to be a Millionaire?," and its challenger, blatantly titled "Greed: The Multi-Million Dollar Challenge," as well as the mega-popular voyeuristic "Survivor" with its numerous copy-cat competitors, reflects the mind-set of the culture,[26] as does the "epidemic of U.S. obesity," which, in large part, is a product of affluence. The problem was termed a "national emergency" by obesity experts at a conference of the American Obesity Association.[27]

Fresh examples of unbelievable affluence seem to occur daily. Little wonder that a book like James Twitchell's somewhat blasphemous *Lead Us into Temptation* is well received. Twitchell argues that America's true religion is shopping, and that this is good. Shopping, he says, is how Americans achieve meaning; the accumulation of possessions, since they define our identity, is the way fulfillment is found. "Salvation through consumerism is not a contradiction, but a necessity."[28]

Only in an incredibly affluent society!

Education for Excellence?

Sir John also postulated that the Age of Affluence creates increased educational possibilities, but that in the ensuing Age of Intellect, the primary focus of obtaining an education is on achieving personal advancement and wealth. Education critics see such advancement as a major goal in the quest for education today, largely as the result of the impact of John Dewey whose humanistic theories, accepted and implemented at the mid-nineteenth century and since, have in the opinion of many led to the sorry state of public education in the U.S. today.

Dewey believed that instead of merely training children in the virtues and preparing them for their place in society, education should be egalitarian, giving each child his opportunity to advance in society without regard to ability or effort. Ostensibly a noble goal, it can easily be corrupted into a drive for personal enrichment.

"[T]he parchment given to several million youngsters each June may be a passport to work, but it is often merely printed proof of the failure of higher education."—Martin Gross

---

Interestingly, in the same magazine in which Dewey's impact on the American educational system was considered, an advertisement for a Christian university asked in bold type, "What could your family do with an extra $27,975 a year?" The data cited indicated that a particular degree would produce that much more income.[29]

Martin L. Gross, best-selling author of *The End of Sanity,* deplores the decline of well-rounded education in America's institutions of higher learning in favor of "politically correct" elective courses whose major function is to make possible graduation and employment. He writes: "[The New Establishment] has now virtually completed its conquest, much to the distress of those who remember the colleges—when. The result is that the parchment given to several million youngsters each June may be a *passport to work*, but it is often merely printed proof of the failure of higher education" (emphasis mine).[30]

Against this backdrop of affluence and so-called pragmatic education, let's see if there is in the United States today evidence of the characteristics which Sir John Glubb identified as being present in the declining days of former empires.

On Guard We Stand

Has the United States, in spite of its global superpower status, pulled back into a de facto defensive mode? Many observers and military analysts think so. We're told that the United States spends twice as much on defense as China, Russia, North Korea, Iraq, Iran and Libya combined.[31] What are the evidences the analysts cite for concluding that the "last-stage characteristic" of defensiveness is in view in America?

In a *Washington Post* article entitled "The Impotence of Omnipotence," Daniel Johnson noted that the U.S. is not currently (2000) acting like a superpower, but instead exhibits impotence and ambivalence in its foreign policy. Beyond the confidence-in-leadership crisis exacerbated by the Clinton/Lewinsky affair, there appears to be little purpose or resolve in foreign issues.

Johnson writes,

> For example, nobody doubts that America has the power to topple Saddam Hussein. Yet the United States has consistently pulled punches. Foreign observers assume that the United States is either weak-willed or has a hidden agenda to keep Hussein in place.

The strong leadership that led to the dismantling of communism in Eastern Europe has disappeared, and the vacuum left has been filled only with misfired rhetoric.[32]

The growing conviction is that more than just the will is lacking. A 1999 *WORLD* magazine cover story indicated that with more threats around the world than ever, the mighty U.S. military of the 1980s is long gone.

After communism imploded in 1989, the crack Cold War U.S. force began to be systematically dismantled and carted off like the rubble from the Berlin Wall. Washington slashed troop strength, mothballed hardware and dynamited defense spending. [During the Clinton administration, the budget was balanced, in large measure, through massive cuts in military expenditures.] The resulting strain on U.S. military assets has experts reexamining the readiness of American forces—and finding it lacking.

According to House Armed Services Committee members, the U.S. Army in 1992 could field eighteen divisions; in 1999, it could muster only ten. During the same period, fighter air wings were trimmed from twenty-four to thirteen. The Navy, which aspired to a 600-ship fleet during the Cold War, now sails with just over 300. The Army is $1.7 billion short of basic ammunition. The Marine Corps, America's 911 force, is $193 million shy.

All of this is occurring in a global political climate more volatile than during the Cold War. Rogue nations like Iran, Iraq and North Korea are stockpiling military weapons and technology courtesy of Russia and China. Pakistan and India have developed nuclear bombs. Chinese forces, after helping themselves to U.S. intelligence, are building missiles that threaten the U.S. And military volcanoes around the planet have continued to erupt with regularity: Kuwait, Somalia, Haiti, Macedonia, Rwanda, Zaire, Bosnia and Kosovo.

"Most wouldn't tell you," said a retired Air Force colonel who requested that his name be withheld to protect his defense-related post-military job, "but American forces are growing tired of the world police role. Those serving are looking at a rising potential to enter [foreign] conflicts and not make it home. When that happens, a critical element of readiness is affected—*the willingness of the 'doer' to go do it*" (emphasis mine).[33]

With more threats around the world than ever, the mighty U.S. military of the 1980s is long gone.

Female Power

In addition to the major cutbacks in military budgets, there are other disconcerting factors at play, including the feminization of the military. Wesley Prudens, editor-in-chief of *The Washington Times*, writes that "[o]ur mighty military, no longer designed to be a war-fighting machine, has already surrendered to the [feminists] and the lady-men in Congress. Several politically incorrect officers at the Pentagon concede that the signs are ominous."[34]

Martin Gross documents the feminization trend. West Point, Annapolis and the Air Force Academy have all gone coed, with coed barracks at the Point. The result is a deterioration in the leadership quality of recent graduates, according to field commanders who have characterized them as too often being "weenies."

Over the past decade, female power in the military has continually expanded. In 1991, the Air Force, despite opposition, permitted women to fly combat planes. The Navy now permits all women sailors to go on combat duty, and they are being deployed on numerous ships (excluding submarines, though a strong push to include subs is underway), despite the proven widespread sexual problems of adultery and pregnancy and the lack of physical strength that a combat emergency aboard ship might require.

Desert Storm showed that women are not as easily deployable as men. In fact, their presence in a battle zone can be a liability. The nondeployable rate [meaning they weren't ready for duty] was three to four times higher among women, not counting higher rates of voluntary and involuntary discharges because of pregnancy or child-care concerns.

The pregnancy problem is not inconsequential, especially considering the increased sexual contact between men and women soldiers, sailors and airmen, married or unmarried. Of the 360 women who returned from Desert Storm aboard the *USS Acadia* (dubbed *The Love Boat*), thirty-six (ten percent) were pregnant, evidence of considerable sexual activity in the ranks.[35]

Prudens explains how the feminization of the military is a major part of the reason why all of the services, except for the Marines, are having severe difficulty in finding recruits. He writes:

War, though hell it certainly is, has nevertheless drawn young men to it from the dawn of history, and the warrior culture, by definition, is male. When young men are told that fighting wars is something that women can do as well as men, a lot of young men who would otherwise be drawn to a warrior career say "to h— with it." Army recruiters have to make up the slack with more women, which further changes the culture, which further repels young men, which requires recruiting more women, which . . . you get the idea.[36]

A cartoon by Walter Stayskal of the *Tampa Tribune* graphically summarizes the situation. In the first panel, captioned "The Good Old Days," an Army recruiting center is filled with people. Outside it is a sign with a forceful Uncle Sam pointing his finger and saying, "I want you." The second panel, "Nowadays," shows an empty recruiting center. The sign outside has a worried-looking Uncle Sam on his knees in a prayerful attitude saying, "Please join up."[37]

Nor does the foregoing consider the major concern of top veteran military leadership over the Clinton enforcement of homosexual involvement in the military, a practice previously prohibited. Morale has suffered seriously as a result. The status of the U.S. military became one of the issues in the 2000 presidential race, with George W. Bush and many military leaders claiming that its strength had seriously declined.

It does appear that America may now be illustrating Sir John's words: "[H]istory seems to indicate that great nations [in decline] do not normally demilitarize from motives of conscience, but rather because of the weakening of a sense of duty in citizens, and the increase of selfishness manifested in the desire for wealth and ease."[38]

"Give Me Your Masses . . ."

The influx of foreigners into the capital and other major cities of an empire is "one of the oft-repeated phenomena in empire life cycles," according to Sir John. Particularly is this true in the latter stages of the cycle.

How does the United States stack up in this regard?[**]

According to *Stimulus* magazine, the United States receives more immigrants in a year than all other nations of the world combined. The population of over fifty major U.S. cities will be predominantly immigrants and/or ethnic minorities by the end of the year 2000.[39]

** In quoting information on U.S. immigration statistics and procedures, I am not making a personal statement about the effect of such immigration. Neither is this a prejudice against any race, nor an endorsement of every conclusion reached in the quotations. It is simply an attempt to show that major immigration is occurring.

In the last generation, the immigrant population in the United States has tripled from 9.6 million in 1970 to 26.3 million in 1988. The non-profit Center for Immigration Studies reports that nearly one in every ten U.S. residents is an immigrant, that one in seven immigrants lives in poverty and that the welfare recipients among them is thirty to fifty percent higher than among native-born.[40]

Immigration is a hotbed of controversy in America, according to Alan Wolfe, sociology professor at Boston University and nationally known author. In his book, *One Nation After All,* Wolfe claims (as a result of the extensive interviews that formed the basis of his book) that most Americans resolve the conflict over whether or not to limit immigration by drawing a distinction between "good" immigrants and "bad" immigrants. Good immigrants are those who enter the country legally and are paying their way. By welcoming these immigrants, middle-class Americans confirm their commitment to humanitarianism, not to mention a steady source of labor for less-than-pleasant jobs. Illegal immigrants, on the other hand, are not welcomed by most Americans. The 1998 California Proposition 187 (to expel illegal immigrants) demonstrated this, and majorities outside California (sixty-three percent) agreed.

As for multiculturalism, Americans favor a benign brand of multiculturalism, i.e., teaching respect for other cultures. Another California proposition revealed that a majority of Californians believe that people should retain their culture and language.[41]

Martin Gross points out that through what he terms "New Establishment" influence there has been a dramatic change in the composition of immigrants being accepted in America. In fact, he writes, since the composition of the immigrant group has changed so dramatically, many worry about the future ethnic makeup of the nation.

As demographers tell us, the European base that founded America and established its mores is changing so rapidly that by the year 2040, European-Americans—from Anglos to Irish to Germans to Poles to Jews—will become a minority *if* major changes are not made quickly. . . .

Except for Native Americans, the U.S. is obviously a nation of immigrants. But as the composition of the [current] immigrant group changes dramatically, many worry about the future ethnic makeup of the nation . . . can the new immigrants be as easily absorbed into our Anglo-American culture?

How much of the fear about the new immigration is well-founded and how much of it is the result of paranoia?

The trigger for the dissatisfaction is threefold:

1. The ethnic mix of new immigrants has been heavily skewed away from Europeans (who are now restricted to a lottery to enter) toward Mexicans, Latin Americans, Asians and those of Caribbean origin.

2. Of the legal immigrants who arrive here, too many are not an asset to the nation, but have instead become a financial burden to taxpayers.

3. The invasion of illegal immigrants is costing us billions and bringing in too many people who are uneducated and find it difficult to assimilate.

All three fears are reasonable.[42]

FAIR, the Federation of Americans for Immigration Reform, states that "at the present rate, immigration will soon reach 13 million per decade . . . [largely because of] the policy of 'family reunification,' which triggered vastly increased immigration, especially of those with less education and fewer skills. [Then] the Immigration Act of 1990 resulted in an increase in the total numbers of immigrants by some 40 percent, most of them from Third World countries."

FAIR shows that immigrants (often including illegals) actually receive far more government aid than citizens who pay the bill—

forty-seven percent more in the majority of cases. Gross indignantly points out that "[i]t is rather unthinkable but true. A child born to a pregnant illegal immigrant is not only *not* deported back to the country of origin with the mother, but the baby automatically becomes a citizen of the United States" (emphasis in original).[43]

> In 1996, in California alone, 100,000 children of illegal alien mothers became automatic citizens, with some 250,000 nationwide. Each became eligible for AFDC welfare benefits which include a sizeable monthly cash payment, plus food stamps. A $3,000 hospital bill is automatically paid by taxpayers.
>
> The mother, instead of being deported as an illegal alien, is given permanent residency, since she is now the mother of an American. (Where the father is known, he too is generally given immigration protection.) The once-impoverished woman, often unmarried, can now receive, as the mother of an American citizen, housing aid and WIC (extra nutrition for an infant child and mother in the form of vouchers).
>
> When the child grows up, he or she can use the citizenship granted at birth to "reunite" the family in America under a "family reunification" act. This also includes the extended families, in what the INS refers to as "Chain Immigration" with no theoretical end point.[44]

The regulations seem bizarre, and the situation is only the tip of the iceberg. Gross documents the fact that the immigration problem can only grow exponentially and that the burden to the taxpayer is already intolerable. Little wonder that he titled his book, *The End of Sanity*. He lays the blame for the insanity in this area of American public policy and life (as well as in a number of others) at the doorstep of what he calls "the New Establishment"—leadership intent on creating an "experimental" society based on unproven, destabilizing concepts.

Regardless of why or how it is happening, however, the recent immigration picture in America does look suspiciously like the scene at the end-stage of past empires as Sir John found it to be.

Hallelujah! We're on the Dole!

The welfare state. Sir John observed that history indicates that the Age of Decline of a great nation is often a period which shows a tendency toward the provision of welfare of one sort or another. So what is the welfare situation in America at the turn of the twenty-first century?

Boston University sociology professor, Alan Wolfe, discovered in extensive interviews that while middle-class citizens are not opposed to the principle of welfare, they are against it in its current state. Though fifty-seven percent believe that the country has a responsibility to the poor, the majority do not believe welfare is a right.[45]

The welfare-reform legislation enacted in 1996 sought to move people off of the welfare rolls and into jobs. One of the provisions of the Act, called "charitable choice," made it possible for churches to participate in welfare programs. Obviously welfare reform was, and is, needed.[46]

The Age of Decline of a great nation is often a period which shows a tendency toward the provision of welfare of one sort or another.

Unfortunately, the sort of indiscriminate welfare alluded to in the previous section is typical. Gross comments:

> Never before has so much money been redistributed to the poor through eighty inefficient, overlapping, poorly designed, and bureaucratic federal welfare programs. Yet despite $3 trillion expended to date, poverty has reached an all-time high.
>
> According to the Congressional Research Service, the amount of welfare has now passed $400 billion a year (more than $300 billion

federal and over $100 billion from the states) to feed, house, clothe, heal, and educate the poor—the largest category of government expenditure by far. [This does not include Medicare or Social Security.]

Welfare was supposed to raise millions out of poverty. Instead, after an expenditure of three trillion dollars, it has accomplished exactly the opposite. It has, for example, actually retarded marriage, forcing women to remain single and produce children out-of-wedlock in order to qualify for Washington's check.

In retrospect, welfare has been one of the most debilitating programs in the history of Western society, an anti-charity move that masquerades as beneficence. Like Christmas turkeys from a reborn Scrooge, it is a palliative that does take from the comfortable (or once comfortable), but does not increase the earning power of the poor.[47]

It's different than the welfare corn and free passes to the gladiatorial fights handed out in the final days of Rome, but basically the principle is the same. Gross's summary statement on U.S. welfare may be debated in some of its conclusions, but there is unquestionably the ring of truth in it: "American Marxism, in the form of welfare and supposed redistribution of wealth, has been the greatest curse for the poor in the modern era, keeping the underclass down to provide a constant case study for New Establishment professionals."[48]

In Chapters 7 and 8 we will take a look at the increasingly dominant role of women in society and the heroes of this era, then attempt to find our place in the cultural life cycle and suggest a response.

Endnotes

1. Sir John Glubb, *The Fate of Empires* (Edinburgh: William Blackwood & Sons, Ltd., 1981), 7.

2. *London Times*, reported in *The Calgary Herald*, August 17, 1999, B9.

3. *USA Today*, May 23, 2000, 16C.

4. *Financial Post,* October 12, 2000, C3.

5. *The Calgary Sun,* September 24, 1999, 6.

6. Kevin Kelly, "The Roaring Zeros," *Wired*, September 1999, 151-154.

7. TIME, July 20, 1999, 17.

8. *The Calgary Herald*, November 18, 1999, A8.

9. *Newsweek*, October 25, 1999, 12.

10. *The Calgary Herald*, November 17, 1999, A1.

11. *The Calgary Herald*, November 9, 1999, A1.

12. *The National Post,* September 8, 1999, A1.

13. *Financial Post,* October 3, 2000, C1.

14. *U.S. News and World Report*, July 31, 2000, 45-46.

15. *The Calgary Herald*, October 30, 2000, E5.

16. "Performance Cuisine," *Newsweek*, August 17, 1999, 60-61.

17. *The Calgary Herald,* September 14, 2000, A24.

18. *The National Post*, November 30, 2000, A3.

19. *AAA World*, November-December 1999, 6-8.

20. *The Calgary Herald*, November 26, 1999, LS1.

21. Celeste McGovern, "It's a Dog's Life," *The Report*, February 5, 2001, 52-53.

22. *National Post,* February 5, 2001, A1-2.

23. *WORLD*, August 7, 2000, 14.

24. *Newsweek,* September 15, 1999, 51.

25. *The Financial Post,* September 27, 2000, C2.

26. *The Calgary Herald,* September 24, 2000, C2.

27. Ibid., November 21, 1999, A9.

28. Gene Edward Veith, "Money Mysticism," review of *Lead Us into Temptation, WORLD*, July 14, 1999, 26.

29. An advertisement in *WORLD*, July 31, 1999, 80.

30. Martin Gross, *The End of Sanity* (New York: Avon Books, 1998), 109.

31. *Harpers*, February 1997, 3.

32. Daniel Johnson, "The Importance of Omnipotence," *Washington Post Weekly,* November 30, 1998, 21.

33. *WORLD*, May 29, 1999, 14-20.

34. Wesley Prudens, editorial in *The Washington Times,* November 25, 1999, 18.

35. Gross, 98-103.

36. Prudens, 18.

37. *Tampa Tribune* cartoon, as reproduced in *WORLD*, March 20, 1999, 13.

38. Glubb, 12.

39. *Stimulus*, Spring 1997, 3.

40. Gabriel Escobar, "Transforming a Nation in Just One Generation," *Washington Post Weekly*, January 18, 1999, 29.

41. Alan Wolfe, *One Nation After All* (New York: Viking, 1998), 132-150.

42. Gross, 251-262.
43. Ibid., 270-271.
44. Ibid., 273.
45. Wolfe, 186.
46. TIME, August 25, 1997, 40-48.
47. Gross, 55-56, 157.
48. Ibid., 57.

Chapter Seven

Women—Equal or Superior?

*Women are entering everywhere where men
once pursued masculine rituals, even the military.*

—Martin L. Gross in *The End of Sanity*

Can a woman win the White House? queries a headline in *George* magazine.

Strawberry Saroyan is author of the above-mentioned article. In it she reports on a group announcing its support for a female presidential candidate by 2008 and concludes that it could happen. She quotes a University of Chicago study which reveals that ninety percent of the populace is ready to vote female. Apparently "hard research shows that the fight for equal opportunity in the political arena has largely been won. . . . "[1] And, of course, since Hillary Clinton's 2000 election to the Senate, speculation over her run for the presidency in 2004 has become rife.

"Women Will Rule New Millennium: Poll" was the bold and startling headline for another article which reported on a major survey conducted in mid-1999 by the Chicago-based Billennium Organizing

Committee. Fifty-six percent of the respondents thought a woman would lead the U.S. in the next century (now this century). "Women are coming into their own with regards to leadership," said Mark Mitten, president of Billennium.[2]

Is this an indication that another of the characteristics of an empire's decline—a growing dominance by women—is upon us?

Feminism on the March

There is no question that the feminist movement has had a major impact on American culture in the past century. Warren Farrell, author of *Why Men Are the Way They Are,* seems to have conceded a feminist victory, commenting, "People have said that we have been engaged in a war of the sexes, but that's not true. It's a one-sided war, and the men haven't shown up yet."[3] And according to Christina Hoff Sommers, author of *The War Against Boys,* unless strong resistance to the current trend occurs, it is going to get much worse in the future because of continuing major changes in education.

Sommers documents extensive feminist-led efforts to "correct" the alleged male bias in schools and "overhaul" the social condition of boys to make them more like girls. She

- exposes the dishonest pseudo-scholarship behind the myth of American girls as victimized and "silenced"
- proves beyond doubt that it is boys, not girls, who are on the weak side of an educational gender gap
- documents the frightening anti-boy prejudice that flourishes in most public schools
- reveals the totalitarian-style program *already being used* to reconstruct boys' "gender identity," beginning in kindergarten (emphasis in the original), and

- shows how the decline in boys' academic achievement and the increase in their anti-social behavior have their roots in the flawed educational approaches of the past thirty years.

More than this, she proves exhaustively that the claims of Carol Gilligan, Harvard-based "matron saint of girl advocates and radical feminists" [claims taken as gospel by liberal journalists, legislators and school officials] are utterly baseless—with Gilligan adamantly refusing to release to the public even the minimal data she has used to support her claims. Sommers also details how Gilligan's "research" is typical of that of the anti-male movement.

While Sommers does present constructive suggestions on how to counteract the trend, *The War Against Boys* is primarily an alarming indictment of a pervasive anti-male movement in the nation's educational system. As such, it is not only a call to recognize both the present and potentially far greater future danger of this feminist assault, but an earnest appeal to stand against it.[4]

But while the drive to make boys into girls is dangerous, on the other side of the coin, Martin Gross is convinced that the push to move women into traditional male roles is even more harmful. Faulting the politically correct New Establishment for promoting the feminist position, Gross says,

> Unfortunately, much of the excessive push in favor of women is not only to the detriment of men, but is also upsetting the balance to everyone's disadvantage.
>
> For the New Establishment to unfairly push women forward and limit men through modern sex bias may be a social experiment of great titillation and fashionability. But it is also one that *toys too frivolously, and dangerously, with the destiny of Western society* (emphasis mine).[5]

In a chapter entitled, "American Women: Darlings of the New Establishment," Gross documents the effects of the feminists' offensive and the politically current mind-set. He shows how in the medical, legal, political and military fields, women are either gaining dominance or making major inroads.

While he emphasizes that "gender should be absolutely no barrier to achievement, at any level, up through the chance to produce great scientific work or even gain the Presidency of the United States," he maintains that the current situation has violated all good sense and decency. How? Through granting women special advantage in test scores and admission to professional schools, as well as assorted "Achievement Charity" ranging from false designation as National Merit Scholars, or having to do fewer push-ups (and meet lesser requirements) in the military, to weaker academic requirements, to misdirected medical specialties and to (harmful) changes in the teaching of law.[6]

Gross' book is extremely well documented. However, the point isn't whether or not he is correct in all of his conclusions, though they are carefully supported. The fact is that women are steadily moving in the direction the current feminist agenda has clearly set out—not merely equality, but superiority.

The Agenda Is Being Met

Christopher Caldwell, writing in *Weekly Standard* under the title, "The Feminization of America," claims that Hillary Clinton is engaged in "welcoming men to their new role as the second sex." Says Caldwell,

> She and other feminists are doing their best to convince us that women are now the "first sex." Clinton doesn't want us using the word "feminization," however, preferring the more plausible "maturing of politics" or "humanization of society." Such views notwithstanding,

appealing to women as a group has become a driving force of our culture. And, whatever else it means, feminization is a *radical* force. (emphasis mine)[7]

"Tomorrow's Second Sex" was the title of an in-depth *Economist* article which indicated that "[c]rime and unemployment statistics show [the] clear trend in the Western world [that] men are failing. . . ." The article cited statistics which revealed that between 1980 and 1992 women accounted for two-thirds of the increase in the workforce, while male unemployment increased. The future for men appears bleak since the fastest-growing areas already employ mostly female workers: residential care seventy-nine percent, data processing sixty-eight percent, health services seventy percent and child care seventy percent. Unfortunately, one of the consequences of the increasing unemployability of men is a rise in crime—eighty-seven percent of all violent crime in the U.S. is perpetuated by males, mostly under twenty-four.[8]

The future for men appears bleak since the fastest-growing areas already employ mostly female workers.

The charge that feminists are altering the laws of the land is made in the article "Feminism vs Free Speech," in *American Enterprise* magazine, which gives a summary of *Feminist Jurisprudence: Equal Rights or Neo-Paternalism?* by Michael Weiss and Cathy Young.

Because radical feminists think "such key concepts of Western jurisprudence as judicial neutrality and individual rights" are "patriarchal fictions designed to protect male privilege," they have sought to change many of America's laws. Although they have been strikingly successful, they have "done severe damage to America's legal system" in the process. Examples are in the area of sexual harassment, stalking and battered women syndrome, in which the "courts [have been used] to abolish male privilege while preserving and expanding female privilege."[9]

Thus, some observers of the culture are convinced that the feminists' victories are of questionable value, at best, and extremely harmful at worst. Suzanne Fields writes in *Insight*: "Feminism has opened doors at work, and closed doors at home. . . . So while feminism has clearly created new work opportunities for women, its effect on the home has not been positive. It has generated a whole new set of worries for parents and causes women to feel torn between the demands of a public self and the desires of a private self."[10]

"The Wages of Women's Lib," an article in *World & I* by Elizabeth Fox-Genovese, explores what feminism has done to marriage. Her conclusions are disconcerting:

> Feminists don't like to admit it, but they don't think very highly of marriage. . . . From the very beginning of the feminist movement in the 1800s, marriage reform has been one of their goals. Early on they advocated a woman's right to own property, to divorce, and to retain custody of her children. These seem like reasonable, modest goals to us today, partly because we have forgotten that historically, marriage vows caused a woman to forfeit, for the most part, her independent standing in society.
>
> By the 1960s marriage laws had changed almost beyond recognition . . . [but] not satisfied with these dramatic changes, the feminist goal shifted from the reforming of marriage to its abolition. They use the term "liberation" and agitate as enthusiastically for no-fault divorce and single motherhood as they did for abortion on demand.
>
> It is now clearer than ever that the greatest victims of the collapse of marriage are children, but the statistics also reveal that divorce (and even more so the decision not to marry in the first place) harms men

more than it does women. Though women may suffer financially, men sustain more physical and emotional damage. Thus by attacking marriage, feminists are *striking a blow at the health of society as a whole* (emphasis mine).[11]

At What Price?

The success of the drive to rid society of marriage is having dire consequences according to an article in *Family in America*. Statistics show traditional families in decline, while government-subsidized (via welfare) "alternative lifestyles" proliferate. Unwed motherhood rose from 5.3 percent of all U.S. births in 1960 to 30.1 percent in 1992.[12]

> ## "[T]he feminist goal shifted from the reforming of marriage to its abolition."—Elizabeth Fox-Genovese

The dire consequences of the shift is echoed even in the viewpoint of radical feminist, Susan Faludi, whose book, *Stiffed: The Betrayal of the American Man*, posits that contemporary men suffer from isolation and the lack of a communal role. This leaves them to validate themselves only with turgid displays of muscles or with wealth and material possessions.

While Ms. Faludi's book was drubbed by critics for its facile analysis and its failure to attach sufficient blame to the social effect of her own feminist ideals, recent research confirms a crisis. More than twenty-seven million American children live without their father; more than one-third are unlikely to see him even once a year, according to the Missouri-based National Center for Fathering. U.S. Department of Justice data reveals that seventy-two percent of adolescent murderers, sixty percent of rapists, and seventy percent of long-term prisoners grew up in father-absent homes. A 1994 study in the *American Journal of Public Health* reported that children exhibiting violent misbehavior in schools were eleven times as likely to live without their father as children who did not misbehave.[13]

And so the story goes. It appears that no area of life is immune when one considers that demands are made in the name of feminism for women to be included on male teams in sports like hockey and football, sometimes involving lawsuits being brought for the right.

Women of the Cloth

There is also a growing demand by women for leadership roles in religious affairs in both traditional and nontraditional groups. Within Christendom, it has been most evident among theologically liberal churches, but it is also an issue in the ranks of conservative groups as well. Not only are a growing number of women serving as ministers, but, according to Brian Abshire, writing in *Chalcedon Report*, many pulpits today are being filled by "girlie-men." He describes how numerous churches have substituted seminary education for godly character, often ordaining to the ministry "those who don't think or act like men, but who have adopted an essentially feminine view of life." This "feminization of the clergy" has led to failure to confront sin boldly, to the pursuit of peace at any price and to a watering down of the biblical message.[14]

Even modern witches are said to be winning the fight for religious rights and recognition. Hundreds from the U.S. attended the 1999 World Parliament of Religions in South Africa and "were accepted into the multi-faith fold without a fuss." Witches staffing a "Pagans from the USA" booth boasted that U.S. witches now number up to one million, and "with Wicca you don't put your strength in God. You put your strength in yourself. You worship the Earth, the air, water, you know, all that good stuff."[15]

And then there's the goddess—or Lilith—the focus of a series of fairs and popular music events presented by female musicians and female-led groups. The mythical raven-haired Lilith, considered by her supporters to be the first feminist, is supposed to have been the wife of Adam—and his equal—created from the Earth, as he was, "when God realized he had made a mistake in creating the first man." The legend, one of many, incorporates demonism, the occult, lesbian imagery and misapplied Scripture. While worthwhile organizations, such as the Breast Cancer Fund, have been supported by Lilith Fair earnings, so has Planned Parenthood. Condoms were dispensed at all concerts.[16]

The Glass Ceiling and "Dumb" Males

The glass ceiling in business after business continues to shatter. Fairly typical is the fact that a woman now heads Barclays Global Investors, the world's largest money manager with more than $1 trillion in assets under management.[17] More than half the federal public service is female, and more than half of all executive, administrative, scientific and professional positions are held by women.[18]

The U.N., whose influence and power in the U.S. is eagerly promoted by many, proposes women's rights, including the right to abortion and parent-free access to reproductive services for adolescents. Since the U.N. makes no allowance for any who oppose abortion, for example, governments that recognize these and other similar rights are expected to declare individuals (such as clergy) who speak out against such rights to be human-rights violators.[19]

Woman reigns—even on the comics page. While wisecracks about a woman's inability to parallel park or the proverbial "dumb blonde" (unfortunately sometimes unkindly uttered) are now politically incorrect, the "dumb dad" jokes are more popular than ever. The "Blondie and Dagwood" strip is now just "Blondie," after the heroine. "Hi and

Lois," "Adam" (house husband) and more—all reflect the poor dopey pop and the smart mom.[20]

In TV and the movies, it's "dumb and dumber" for dad and other assorted males. *Psychology Today* reported on a survey which revealed that current attitudes toward men and women have changed exponentially from those expressed in a 1970 survey: "Clearly, women's images have improved while men's have, uh, gone south. Women were characterized as intelligent, logical, independent, adventurous, and good at relationships. Men were rated as not as knowledgeable, objective or assertive as in the 1970s."[21]

"Turning Boys into Girls," an article by Michelle Cottle in *Washington Monthly*, reveals that men are—to the delight of feminists—becoming far more obsessed with their physical appearance. Over $3.5 billion was spent by men on toiletries in a recent year, twenty percent of men get manicures, and eighteen percent have skin treatments like mud packs, according to the magazine *Men's Health*.[22]

And we could go on.

A Disclaimer

Let me make one thing very clear. I am not a male chauvinist. I do not condone the inequities which women have suffered over the centuries. I do not believe for a moment that women are in any way inferior to men as persons. I agree with Martin Gross that gender should not be a barrier to equal pay for equal work or to advancement. What has been presented above is simply a brief look at the indicators in our society that reveal a strong drive for dominance for women. As one writer succinctly put it: "[Ultra] feminism is a radical force, implying a remaking of society and a rejection of ideas as old as the Bible."[23]

Sir John would undoubtedly suggest it's one more of the characteristics of "end game for the empire."

Women—Equal or Superior?

Endnotes

1. Strawberry Saroyan, "Can a Woman Win the White House?" *George,* February 1999, 94-97.

2. *The Calgary Herald,* September 23, 1999, A1.

3. *Patriarch*, January 1997, 6.

4. *Conservative Book Club Review,* July 2000.

5. Martin Gross, *The End of Sanity* (New York: Avon Books, 1998), 106.

6. Ibid., 68-106.

7. Christopher Caldwell, "The Feminization of America," *Weekly Standard*, December 23, 1996, 14-19.

8. "Tomorrow's Second Sex," *Economist*, September 28, 1998, 23-26.

9. "Feminism vs Free Speech," *American Enterprise,* November/December 1996, 96.

10. Suzanne Fields, *Insight*, January 26, 1995, as reported in *Current Thoughts and Trends,* September 1995, 9-10.

11. Elizabeth Fox-Genovese, "The Wages of Women's Lib," *World & I,* November 1997, 32-37.

12. Alan Tapper, "Do Families Fare Well Under the Welfare State?" *Family in America*, July 1997, 1-7.

13. Marnie Ko, "The Masculinity Muddle," *The Report,* November 22, 1999, 41.

14. Brian Abshire, "Girlie-men in the Pulpit," *Chalcedon Report*, February 1998, 6-8.

15. *The National Post,* December 10, 1999, A14.

16. J.M. Smith, "Secrets of the Lilith Fair," *National Liberty Journal*, June 1999, 9.

17. *The Calgary Herald*, November 25, 1999, D4.

18. *The Calgary Herald,* December 7, 1999, A1.

19. Diane Sabom and Frances Kissling, "Is the UN Women's Agenda Riding Roughshod over Religion?" *Insight,* September 6, 1999, 40-43.

20. Kevin Michael Grace, "Neutered in Newsprint," *The Report,* November 8, 1999, 44.

21. *Psychology Today*, November/December 1998, 8.

22. Michelle Cottle, "Turning Boys into Girls," *Washington Monthly*, May 1998, 32-36.

23. Ted Byfield, editorial, *The Report,* November 9, 1999, 48.

Chapter Eight

Our Star-Studded Heroes

How Julia finally joined the $20M club
—Newspaper headline

Columnist Leonard Pitts, Jr., recently noted: "My middle son, Marlon, complained to me just the other day that his generation is coming of age 'in a world without heroes.' " Pitts said, "His words tugged at me. . . . Our children have learned to wait for the other shoe to drop, for 'heroes' to be unmasked and values betrayed."[1]

But is it true that this generation has no heroes?

Radio talk-show super host, Dr. Laura Schlessinger, cited a 1999 study that showed high school students four-to-one in favor of acquitting President Bill Clinton of perjury even though a federal judge pronounced him guilty of lying under oath.

"We elected the president to be our economic and policy leader," one student explained, "not to be a role model. I want him to run the country. For role models and heroes, we can look to sports stars or Mother Teresa."

"Sports stars," gasped Dr. Laura. "Names like Sprewell (basketball star who faced charges for choking his coach), Rodman (bizarre cross-dressing, outrageous-acting egotistic basketball pro) and Tyson (frequently imprisoned and disbarred boxer) come to mind, along with an article in *Sports Illustrated* on the arrogance, violence, domestic abuse, drug abuse, alcoholism and promiscuity (the late Wilt Chamberlain boasted in his autobiography of 20,000 sexual conquests) of many a sports great. *These* are heroes?" (emphasis mine).[2]

Yes, bizarre as it may seem, these and others of their ilk, are indeed modern-day heroes—at least if public figures are deemed to be heroes based on their popularity, income, status, influence and the desire of others to emulate them.

The irony of it is well expressed in an article by Mark Stewart in *The Washington Times*. He writes:

> There was a time when athletes routinely signed autographs for admiring fans. But where have you gone, Joe DiMaggio? The Yankee Clipper played during a simpler time, when heroes, for the most part, lived clean, drank their milk, stayed married to one spouse and generally lived to a ripe old age.
>
> Even the "bad boys" such as James Dean don't quite compare to the anti-hero horrors parents see today. Dean's ducktail hairstyle, leather jacket and rebel image have a milk-and-cookies air about them next to today's "gangsta rappers' " glorification of rape, murder and mayhem.
>
> Yesterday's Joe DiMaggio, Gary Cooper and Fabian are today's Dennis Rodman, Robert Downey Jr. [jailed actor] and Marilyn Manson [shock Satanist singer].
>
> . . . How are parents supposed to guide their children's hero-worshiping impulses when the cultural landscape seems littered with crude, overpaid, oversexed, drug-addled reprobates?
>
> Colorado College sociologist Kathy Ciuffre says, "Heroes are no longer people who reach inside themselves to overcome problems and

do what is right in the face of daunting obstacles. Now they're people who reach for guns and blast somebody."

Violence in the media is one thing, but Richard Wessler, a psychology professor at Pace University in New York, adds that today's "celebrity culture" also has adjusted the way we view "heroes."[3]

Without argument, some of the biggest celebrities today are rock musicians, athletes, actors and actresses. It's one of the reasons why *WORLD*, an unabashedly Christian weekly news magazine, reviews movies. In an article entitled, "Hollywood Heroes," Gene Edward Veith says, "*WORLD* covers movies because, for better or for worse, they are mirrors for our culture's vices, virtues, and pressures, and *they influence* what's coming up next" (emphasis mine).[4]

Without argument, some of the biggest celebrities today are rock musicians, athletes, actors and actresses.

Perhaps no one needs convincing that actors and actresses, musicians (rock, punk rock, heavy metal, death metal, satanic, etc.), and professional athletes are the heroes/celebrities of our age. Nonetheless, let's briefly document this fact, on the basis of their popularity, income, status and influence.

We Are the Popular People

Actors, actresses, musicians and athletes are absolutely everywhere in the media. Their exploits, activities, crimes, misdemeanors, affairs, marriages, divorces, current "main squeezes," salaries, fashions and more are endlessly in view. Their opinions, on a variety of topics in which they usually have absolutely no expertise, are sometimes cited as the "final word" on the subject.

A comment in *Warning: Nonsense is Destroying America* describes this:

> Celebrity is capriciously bestowed, sometimes to a genuine achiever, but too often to an undistinguished or mediocre one. Take the case of Vanna White. Neither an actress nor an entertainer [as such], she became a celebrity for looking pretty and turning letters proficiently, and celebrity brought her a book contract . . . and a fee schedule of $30,000 per speaking engagement.[5]

Television is largely devoted to the promotion of such celebrities. There are, in addition to the regular networks with their celebrity saturation, a variety of specialized networks which focus entirely on music, entertainment or sports. The largest television audience each year watches football's Super Bowl, an event which is preceded by weeks of nonstop hype, much of it focusing on the "heroes" who will play. A similar situation exists in radio.

On a weekly basis, Monday Night Football is one of the major draws, though its popularity has been challenged recently by the telecasts of World Wrestling Federation (WWF) events. WWF bouts are a blend of acting and phony wrestling (not to be confused with the real sport) with dark and even demonic overtones in the combatant's personas. Their popularity is astonishing.

These heroes and heroines of the WWF (who are now usually the kind of characters who used to be the "bad guys," like The Undertaker, Stone Cold Austin, Degeneration X, Road Dogg and The Blue Meanie) have their own web sites, marketing mechanisms, magazines and, of course, thousands upon thousands of fans. WWF collectors cards on these famous—and infamous—superstars of the sports entertainment world are now available in 22kt gold! Chyna, one of the top female wrestlers, is the subject of about a dozen web sites (in addition to her own) created by adoring fans.

The print media is in large part involved in the celebrity/hero promotion business. Every major newspaper has a sports section and an entertainment section, runs a weekly TV magazine and frequently does special features on one or another of the current cultural heroes, and/or the field they represent. Coverage of this sort even dwarfs the regular news which itself often deals with the activities of the stars of sports, stage and screen.

Consider the following incomplete but representative sampling of such coverage.

- The Beatles. In mid-2000 the print media went into a virtual frenzy on the occasion of several Beatle album and movie rereleases. Typical of the numerous full-page (and more) features are these items:

   The Fab Formula. Nearly 40 years ago, a rock 'n' roll band formed in this salty city of Liverpool had a good run of hits, then disbanded in a haze of marijuana smoke and mutual recriminations.

   Today, three decades after the ugly breakup, the Beatles remain a powerful economic force so tightly woven into Britain's cultural fabric that it seems they are as permanent as the Big Ben clock tower and more popular than the monarchy.[6]

   Busy Little Beatles. Thirty-one years after the Beatles ceased to exist as a working band, every little thing about, and by, the Fab Four continues to be white-hot. The band sold 30.2 million records in the '90s alone. This, from an act that has not toured since August 1966, placed them fifth in sales in the decade.[7]

The Hero Worship Factor

Headlines such as the following make it clear that celebrities are virtually worshiped by their fans.

- "Worshiping at the 'cathedral of tennis'—a story on the 2000 Wimbledon tennis tournament"
- "Faithful worship at guitar altar—where the faithful congregate in small clubs or in arenas and stadiums, lighting their Bics like so many hopeful prayer candles"
- "Jimi Hendrix—He became a guitar god for the ages. 'We're continuing to keep his flame alive.' "[8]

Fans of the female wrestler Chyna take this "worship" concept to the extreme in their terminology. Some of the dozens of fan-generated Chyna web sites (ranked in "excellence" by the entertainer herself) are titled "Laura's Dedication to Chyna," "Temple of Chyna," "Best Pictures at the Shrine of Chyna," "A Shrine to the Beautiful Chyna" and more.

Many of the celebrities whom Americans "worship are largely ignorant, rude, arrogant stumblebums."—Bill O'Reilly

---

In his recent book, *The O'Reilly Factor*, Fox/TNN journalist and anchorman Bill O'Reilly cites example after example to show that many of the celebrities whom Americans "worship are largely ignorant, rude, arrogant stumblebums." He writes:

Americans have gone wacky over celebrities, as any tabloid journalist can tell you. News about celebrities sells. When the late *National Enquirer* publisher Gene Pope decided to stop featuring celebrities on the front page of his huge-circulation weekly, sales plunged. Pope learned from experience—the following week celebrity covers were back, and they never left again. As a result of America's fascination with actors, athletes, singers, etc., celebrities exercise vast influence over what people buy, how they vote, even how they think. We idolize people whose own personal lives are total disasters yet who think nothing of giving advice to their fellow Americans on how they should live their lives.[9]

"Hollywood royalty," as the press dubbed them, were credited in large measure with generating much of the support Al Gore received in the 2000 U.S. presidential election. For example, by threatening not to renew her contract, popular talk-show host Rosie O'Donnell "forced" network executives to air, ostensibly against their wishes, a partisan Gore endorsement by Barbra Streisand just the day before the election. A survey by the Pew Research Center for the People and the Press found that fourteen percent of Americans said they would vote for whichever candidate was endorsed by talk-show host Oprah Winfrey. Alexander Rose of the Associated Press said, "As we live in a 'celebrity-obsessed culture,' it should be no surprise to discover that the celebrity has replaced the king or nobleman of centuries past as the shaper of national opinion."[10]

And apparently it doesn't matter how antisocial and violent the celebrity is. The top 2000 MTV Best Video Award went to Eminem, a.k.a. Slim Shady, the best-selling "hottest rapper around," whose sex-obsessed, brutal lyrics were described by *Newsweek* as "profane, violent, misogynistic, homophobic, misanthropic, self-loathing and brilliant."[11]

The largest-ever (522 pages) November 2000 issue of *GQ* magazine carried its annual selection of the "Men of the Year." As one might expect, the dozen or so honorees all came from the sports and entertainment fields—not a scientist, doctor, politician, economist or businessman among them.[12]

The weekly supermarket tabloids, boasting the largest circulations of any publications in America, appear to thrive on the misdemeanors of stars, as do specialty magazines such as *People* (original and teen versions), a plethora of copycat periodicals and a variety of "soap" digests and similar publications. *Sports Illustrated* and its imitators cover the exploits of the star athletes in weekly detail. Books about celebrity heroes often become best-sellers.

Even the major news magazines, such as TIME and *Newsweek,* frequently devote a great deal of attention to such people. When the superstars of basketball, hockey and football—Michael Jordan, Wayne Gretzky and John Elway respectively—retired, enormous coverage was given. Each retirement was a huge total-media event. Movie stars and musicians are also given inordinate amounts of space.

Heroes of the Web

A recent and frightening development is the proliferation of computer games with their hero factor. Most of these games are not innocent amusements. For example, the fact that the game "Doom" was a major factor in the lives of the two high school killers in the Columbine, Colorado massacre has been well documented.

A glance through one of the numerous monthly computer game magazines is a deeply disturbing experience in itself. Such publications are filled with ads displaying occultic or demonic overtones. Titles like "Diablo II," "Cutthroats," "Torment" and "Revenant," with subhead copy: "Jesus rose from the grave to forgive sins. This guy rose to commit them," dominate the dozens of offerings. The full-page ad for one game makes it clear that the fearsome and bizarre characters are to be considered heroic: "Just when you thought there were no more heroes. Think again. Heroes III of Might and Magic—Armageddon's Blade."

The computerized heroine of one series of games, Lara Croft, has numerous web sites and reputedly millions of fans worldwide. New heroes and heroines regularly arise. By the time you read this there will undoubtedly be characters whose popularity will exceed Lara's. And the predictions are for much more, with new and ever more violent games and technologies, such as virtual reality, on tap.[13]

Without doubt, the entertainers are popular—very popular.

And We're Handsomely Rewarded

A hero's status deserves a hero's reward. Right?

And so the movie and TV actors and actresses, musicians and professional athletes command princely paychecks. Consider the following.

In early 1999 *Forbes* magazine listed the 1998 earnings of the top fifty celebrities, beginning with comedian Jerry Seinfeld, the highest earner, at $267 million. Nineteen of the top fifty were actors or actresses; another fifteen were associated with movie or TV production as writers or directors; nine were singers or band members (with the Rolling Stones tops at $57 million); and the remaining seven were athletes, led by Michael Jordan at $73 million. The lowest paid celebrity—No. 50—was boxer Oscar de la Hoya at only $18.5 million. The average income was $56.15 million.[14]

The "salary scale" went up in 1999. Boxer Holyfield earned $50 million for two fights; actress Julia Roberts became the first woman to break the $20-million-for-one-picture barrier—though others were close behind—and Julianna Margulies, a star in the TV show "ER," rejected a $27 million offer for a two-year contract. A number of other show biz people, like twenty-four-year-old Leonardo DiCaprio, Michael Douglas and Tom Hanks, had long since passed the $20 million per picture barrier. Meanwhile, Seattle Mariner's superstar slugger

Ken Griffey, Jr., turned down a $135 million multiyear contract offer, while Sean "Puffy" Combs, the rap superstar, earned a reported $53 million. (And a similar situation in Europe was illustrated by the sale, for $7.78 million, of rights to his forehead by soccer star Michael Schumacher. For the next three years his flame-red Ferrari cap will carry the logo of Deutsche Vermoegens-beratung—obviously in small letters![15])

A number of show biz people had long since passed the $20 million per picture barrier.

In the year 2000, the lid came right off the salary scale. Shortstop Alex Rodriguez was given a ten-year contract worth $252 million. The "obscene" amount was denounced even by baseball writers. Nonetheless, it affected the salaries for baseball stars, moving them to a whole new plateau of income.

We Have Status

In the current U.S. culture, becoming a celebrity often grants immediate status such as being viewed as superior or qualified in a variety of ways and areas which have nothing whatever to do with their acting, singing or athletic ability.

For example, Spice Girl Geri Halliwell (Ginger) was appointed a goodwill ambassador by the United Nations to review progress made since the 1995 Cairo U.N. Summit on Population and Development and to raise awareness about "reproductive health." On a U.N. sex education mission to the Philippines, she reportedly said, at a reproductive health clinic in Manila, "I believe everyone deserves control over their life, and that means control over their fertility and protection against disease and unwanted pregnancies."[16] The popularity gained through being an outrageous pop singer supposedly qualifies a young star to be a respected spokesman for the U.N. on weighty ethical matters involving contraception and abortion (issues for which the U.N. uses the euphemism "reproductive health").

In an article entitled "Pampering the Rich and Famous Stars," Barry Koltnow documents the fact that with celebrity status comes an endless supply of perks. He writes: "Celebrities, both young and old, tell me constantly that the best thing about being famous, besides the overblown salaries, lavish homes and universal adulation, is getting treated like visiting heads of state. . . ."[17]

When Jesse Ventura, a professional entertainer/wrestler, was elected governor of Minnesota in 1998, he instantly became an "authority" on a wide variety of issues, including religion. His numerous national media appearances since, including an interview in *Playboy* magazine, provided him a platform to display his "wisdom," which included thoroughly denigrating Christians. For a time he even toyed with the idea of a run for the presidency.[18]

In a similar vein, during a period in which billionaire entrepreneur Donald Trump was exploring a run for the U.S. presidency, his then-current live-in girl friend—supermodel Melania Knauss—was evaluated in the media as "maybe [proving] to be the perfect political asset," since, according to one headline, she is "charming, easy on the eyes, and likes to keep the conversation light."[19] Singer Elton John, unabashedly and publicly homosexual, was knighted as Sir John, later given a worldwide audience during Princess Diana's funeral, and performs to sold-out audiences.

Even history texts are not beyond the status power of the stars. Sam Donaldson, on ABC's 20/20, April 2, 1999, explored the problem of errors and distortions in school textbooks. One high school history text was shown to have a total of only six lines on George Washington, founder and first president of the nation, but six pages on actress Marilyn Monroe. Donaldson asserted that researchers "couldn't believe their eyes. Page after page of text and pictures galore of the sex goddess, but barely a mention of the leader of the American revolution."[20]

The 1996 history book, *Bring History Alive*, among numerous errors and revisions, omitted historical figures such as Henry Cabot Lodge and the Wright brothers, but prompted students to discuss how pop icon Madonna symbolized modern culture.[21]

Examples could go on endlessly. Consider the incredible adulation poured out on sports stars like home-run king Mark McGwire, runner-up Sammy Sosa or golfing phenomenon Tiger Woods. While these appear to be decent men, their only claim to fame is their ability to hit a ball out of a park or into a hole. Ponder the irony of Ivana Trump (the socialite former wife of The Donald, whose public divorce proceedings, personal problems, extravagances and affairs of the heart were tabloid fodder), writing an advice column in a national weekly paper. Or a whole bevy of Hollywood stars, many of them either married and divorced several times and/or in a " live-in" situation, pontificating on the "immorality" of Special Prosecutor Kenneth Starr's investigation of President Clinton.

Unquestionably, American stars have the kind of status that appears to qualify them to be considered contemporary commentators and heroes in modern times.

And We Have Influence

Yes, indeed, the stars have influence, certainly on youth, but on most other segments of the population as well. In an article in *Youthworker Update*, entitled "How Hollywood Images Are Hurting Our Kids," documentation is provided to show that the media's message is having an effect.

> For years Hollywood's inherent word to young girls has been "thin is in," and millions of teenage girls have learned to hate their bodies as a result. Adolescents, especially girls, are the most vulnerable to this bombardment by Hollywood's "perfect" body images. A Los Angeles social psychologist asserts, "We're evolving toward an unnatural view of beauty, and what real women look like is labeled wrong and unattractive."
>
> The result has been a phenomenal increase in the incidence of fasting, crash diets, obsessive exercise and life-threatening eating disorders such as anorexia and bulimia. In 1976, bulimia and anorexia occurred in 1% or less of high-school and college girls. By 1996, the figure was approaching four percent![22]

The heroines of the silver screen obviously do have influence.

Some of those heroines—the "warrior women"—are also affecting today's society through their ambivalence, according to Michael Ventura, writing in *Psychology Today*. Ventura cites the dualities in heroines like those in "Buffy, the Vampire Slayer," "Xena: Warrior Princess" and "La Femme Nikita."

> Sexy, blonde 20-something Nikita fights demons and terrorists, but while Buffy's hell is around the corner, Nikita lives there, or as it's called, in Station One. Nikita must obey the Station's commands to torture or kill on demand. Here, torture "is disturbing, but the real ugliness is the stylistic flourish with which it is presented, not as a horror but a titillation." The seductive Nikita romances either men or women, although her main attraction is a passive-aggressive male who is both effeminate and masculine. There are no boundaries and ambivalence is the norm.[23]

Ventura's claim that what he calls "heroine addiction" is affecting society certainly appears to have a basis in fact. An article in *The Report* documents the fact that violence among young females is on the rise. Quoted in that article is the April 1998 issue of *Child and Youth Care Forum*, which indicates "an alarming rise in the number of incidents involving females in all forms of aggression and violence."[24] While there are undoubtedly a number of factors which contribute to this trend, the role of warrior heroines is believed to be a major one.

Heroes of the WWF are now usually the kind of characters who used to be the "bad guys."

Teaching Mrs. Tingle was a film produced by the Disney subsidiary, Miramax. It contains a powerful message that feeds on the idea of teen revenge against an unpleasant teacher who gives bad grades. It evoked a strong response. Parental and other groups succeeded in having it withdrawn in a number of U.S. communities, while in Germany the film was banned after a series of copycat attacks on teachers that left one teacher dead.[25] Again, there is far more than this one film factor at play here, but the influence of the movie heroes' philosophy and actions cannot be denied.

In addition, female revenge fantasies are hitting a nerve with moviegoers, according to Anne Kingston, in her article "The Avenging Wife." Kingston cites movies like *The First Wives Club*, which featured a walk-on by Ivana Trump whom some might call the "patron saint of avenging wives." Ivana's trademark battle cry, "Don't get mad, daaarlink, get everything," consistently evoked cheers from women in the audiences.

Double Jeopardy, a more recent movie, stars actress Ashley Judd whose character plots to kill her rotten, philandering husband. Surprisingly, it became a sleeper hit with audiences comprised of sixty percent women. Copycat behavior and crimes by women have occurred.[26]

The dramatic decline in public sexual morality, especially among young women and girls, can be largely attributed to the influence of amoral actresses, a bevy of whom have recently unabashedly, even proudly, opted for unwed motherhood. Two of the most famous of these, Catherine Zeta-Jones and Madonna were lionized by the secular press during their pregnancies and subsequent deliveries. Madonna, whose son was the second highly publicized out-of-wedlock birth, created a virtual firestorm of worldwide publicity with her subsequent multimillion dollar wedding to the second child's father.

The incredible uncritical regard in which Madonna is held by millions of fans, especially young girls—many of whom openly seek to emulate her—has its harmful effect upon morality. Robert Bork cites the reply of a woman who works with unwed teenage mothers, when asked about how to diminish illegitimacy. "Shoot Madonna," she replied.[27]

Much more could be presented in support of the fact that stars do influence people: 1) TV shows glorify witchcraft and pop-culture paganism through poised and well-dressed actresses, with one result being best-selling status for books on witchcraft for teens;[28] 2) the virtually nonstop morally offensive TV network programming which the *American Family Association* [AFA] *Journal* calls a "prime-time filth fest"; 3) over twenty percent of the network dramas and fifty percent of the sitcoms reviewed in December 1999 promoted the homosexual agenda, which, according to AFA, is a fairly typical percentage. Other shows contained many sexual situations.[29]

The movie channels generally are even worse, some offering pornographic fare. Little wonder that the massive and favorable homosexual exposure has created a climate of acceptance for sodomy and lesbianism, and a steady erosion in sexual morality in America.

Oh Marla!

A Chuck Colson experience at the 1990 White House correspondents' dinner puts the hero/heroine adulation into perspective. Colson relates how he was enjoying a predinner reception, renewing friendships with congressmen, senators and columnists. Since almost everyone present was a public figure, there was no pushing or shoving to rub shoulders with the mighty or to seek autographs.

Suddenly a huge commotion arose in the corridor. Colson assumed it must signal the entrance of the President, since he felt that in that crowd no one other than the President could attract such attention. However, when he was able finally to see who was at the center of the mass of bodies, flashbulbs and microphones, he discovered it was not President Bush, but rather a young blonde woman—the coyly smiling Marla Maples, Donald Trump's girlfriend, the "other woman" in his fractured marriage.

As it turned out, Colson was seated at the same table as Marla. Conversation was no problem, however. He writes:

> Marla spent the entire dinner greeting an unending procession of governors, senators, and Hollywood stars who stopped at the table, many deferentially asking for her autograph. . . . Later, a huge spotlight fell on our table. Marla smiled and waved for the applauding crowd. And in the next morning's newspaper stories covering the event, most of the pictures were of Marla.[30]

It is strange indeed when an adulterous young woman is lionized by those in the highest places in the land. Or when a lecherous old man receives massive media coverage because, at age seventy-three, this self-proclaimed creator of America's sexual revolution is sharing his bed with four young beauties whose combined ages scarcely exceed his. Newspaper headlines such as "Original Playboy Back in Action Thanks to Four Girlfriends and Viagra," accompanied the release of *The Century of Sex: Playboy's History of the Sexual Revolution, 1900-1999*, edited and with a foreword by Hefner himself.[31]

We're beginning to look more and more like ancient Rome all the time.

In mid-1999, Jonathan Rosenblum, U.S. correspondent for *The Jerusalem Post* wrote an insightful opinion article in which he observed, "It used to be that the stars played the heroic roles. Today, we idolize the psychopaths [and the sexually 'liberated']." He writes:

> In 1996, the movie *Scream* was a box-office hit. It portrayed in gruesome detail two teenage killers butchering a dozen fellow students and teachers. One of the "heroes" deadpans, towards the end, that he and his partner found that it was more fun to kill friends than strangers. And then in 1999, we witnessed the [massacre at Littleton, Colorado].
>
> Big-name stars once played heroes. Today megastars like Brad Pitt, John Travolta and Leonardo DiCaprio are as likely to play serial killers ("Natural Born Killers"), killers for sport ("Seven"), hit men ("Pulp Fiction"), teenage psychopaths ("The Basketball Diaries"), or violent loners ("Fight Club"). We take on their viewpoint, as their victims whimper and plead.
>
> No clear causal relationship, of course, can be established between "Scream" and Littleton, any more than a clear causal nexus can be shown between air pollution and any particular death. But there is no denying the frequency with which the most savage real-life killings have come to imitate cinematic models.

Most of us intuitively sense that children who watch 40,000 simulated killings on the screen by the time they are 18 or who spend hundreds of hours playing computer games, the object of which is to dismember one's opponent, will lose their horror at the idea of hurting others. And numerous epidemiological studies confirm that intuition.[32]

Unquestionably, the heroes of our era do influence.

We've suggested that America today does have its heroes, and that, based upon their popularity, income, status and influence which we've sought to document briefly those heroes are the athletes, musicians, actors and actresses of our day.

Now, before we move on to Part Four, we'll do a brief review, then check out a few more indications from history of the marks of an empire in its final decline.

Endnotes

1. Leonard Pitts, Jr., as quoted in *Our Daily Bread*, November 12, 1999, 46.

2. Celeste McGoern, ed., "Brave New World," *Alberta Report*, February 22, 1999, 44.

3. Mark Stewart, "The Modern Hero: Where Have You Gone, Joe DiMaggio?" *The Washington Times, National Weekly edition,* August 23, 1999, 26.

4. Gene Edward Veith, "Hollywood Heroes," *WORLD*, March 30, 1999, 17-21.

5. Vincent R. Ruggiero, *Warning: Nonsense Is Destroying America* (Nashville, TN: Thomas Nelson, 1994), 114.

6. *The Calgary Herald,* August 26, 2000, OS1.

7. *National Post,* August 7, 2000, D3.

8. Headlines in *National Post*, July 8, 2000, A0; *Calgary Herald,* September 1, 2000, D1, *National Post,* September 18, 2000, D3.

9. Excerpts from O'Reilly's book posted on the NewsMax.com web site, September 30, 2000.

10. *National Post,* November 6, 2000, A1.

11. "Foul-mouthed Eminem Cleans Up at MTV Video Awards," *Colorado Springs Gazette,* September 8, 2000, A10.

12. *The Calgary Herald,* November 13, 2000, D2.

13. Source: *Internet, PC Gamer*, August 1999, and *Computer Game World*, November 1999.

14. As reported by the Associated Press, *The Patriot News* (Harrisburg, PA), March 9, 1999, A2.

15. Source: *The Sunday Sun* (Calgary, AB), August 1,1999, 13; *The Calgary Herald*, November 13, 1999, E1; *Working Woman*, July/August 1999, 53-54; *Newsweek*, November 8, 1999, 48-49; Reuters, from the Internet, November 10, 1999 and *National Post*, December 12, 2000, A3.

16. Kevin M. Grace, ed., "Eclectica," *The London Times*, as reported in *Alberta Report*, July 12, 1999.

17. Barry Koltnow, "Pampering the Rich and Famous Stars," *The Calgary Herald*, December 17, 1999, E1.

18. *WORLD,* November 8, 1999, 6.

19. *National Post*, November 30, 1999, E3.

20. *The New American*, September 13, 1999, 40.

21. Lynn Vincent, "Whose Standards?" *WORLD*, November 20, 1999, 28-29.

22. "How Hollywood's Images Are Hurting Our Kids," *Youthworker Update*, July 1996, 1.

23. Michael Ventura, "Women Warriors," *Psychology Today*, November/December 1998, 56-61.

24. Candis McLean, "Spare the Rod and Run for Cover," *The Report*, March 1, 1999, 42-45.

25. *The Calgary Herald*, December 1, E1 and December 3, 1999, E9.

26. Anne Kingston, "The Avenging Wife," *National Post,* December 1, 1999, B1.

27. Robert Bork, *Slouching Toward Gomorrah* (New York: Regan Books, 1996), 143.

28. Roy Maynard, "Charmed, I'm Sure," *WORLD*, September 4, 1999, 24-26.

29. *American Family Association Journal*, November/December 1999, 14-17.

30. Charles Colson, *The Body* (Dallas, TX: Word, 1992), 299-300.

31. *The Calgary Herald*, November 20, 1999, ES10 and *Weekend Post,* November 27, 1999, 2.

32. Jonathan Rosenblum, "When Life Bows Before Lifestyle," *The Jerusalem Post*, August 13, 1999, 13.

Chapter Nine

In Addition to Which . . .

I have a heavy heart about America.
American culture seems to me to be sinking toward sunset.

—Carl F. Henry in *Twilight of a Great Civilization*

Time for a quick review. After summarizing Sir John Glubb's analysis of the characteristics of an empire's final stages—defensiveness militarily, massive immigration, a welfare state and the increasingly dominant role of women, all against the backdrop of incredible affluence—we've looked briefly at the growing presence of these indicators in the United States today.

We then considered the fact that the heroes which Sir John identified as being typical of every great power's last days—actors, musicians and athletes—are unquestionably the heroes of present-day America.

But There's More

While the above are the major indicators detailed by Glubb, he and other historians have noted a number of additional signs of "empire end-game." These include frivolity, the weakening of religious influence, divisiveness within the culture and a widespread loss of traditional morality.

In his seventeen-volume classic, *The Decline and Fall of the Roman Empire*, Edward Gibbon concluded that there were five significant factors in her collapse:

1. a rapid increase in divorce
2. a craze for pleasure
3. the building of gigantic armaments while the enemy was within
4. an increase in violence
5. the decline of religion.[1]

How does the current scene in the United States compare?

We're Into Fun and Games

Without doubt, frivolity is a major part of the American cultural make-up at the turn of the century. The nightly talk shows on TV are often the epitome of nonsense. The popularity of so-called and often obscene comedians, the glut of ostensibly comedy movies and the usually vapid conversation of large segments of the population all attest to the fact. The combination of frivolity and a craze for pleasure have become a never-ending though ultimately unsatisfying pursuit of vast multitudes of people.

Frivolity is a major part of the American cultural make-up at the turn of the century.

Charles Colson, in *Against the Night*, comments insightfully:

Decadent Americans, lacking an object in life beyond self, have exhausted themselves in the mistaken notion that multiplying pleasures produces happiness. Summing up [a recent decade], *Newsweek* reported, "Fun became a serious business . . . pursued with a grim vigor. The . . . ideal of recreation was to have MORE fun in LESS time and be DONE WITH IT."

Citing the popular novel and film, *Bright Lights, Big City*, which details a yuppie's endless journey through the bars and hotels of Manhattan in pursuit of pleasure, *Newsweek* observed, "The fact that he never seemed to actually enjoy himself when he was out having fun elucidated a peculiarly [current] notion: that the pursuit of good times could be a joyless function."[2]

It has been suggested that people often seek pleasure to avoid facing what they subconsciously realize to be serious times. Leo Tolstoy, in his monumental *War and Peace*, observed this and wrote,

As the enemy [Napoleon's troops] drew nearer to Moscow, the attitude taken by its inhabitants in regard to their position did not become more serious, but, on the contrary, *more frivolous*, as is always the case with people who see a great danger approaching. At the approach of danger there are always two voices that speak with equal force in the heart of man: one very reasonably tells the man to consider the nature of the danger and the means of avoiding it; the other even more reasonably says that it is too painful and harassing to think of the danger, since it is not in a man's power to provide for everything and escape from the general march of events; and that it is therefore better to turn aside from the painful subject till it has come, and to think of what is pleasant. In solitude a man generally yields to the first voice; in society to the second. So it was now with the inhabitants of Moscow. It was long since there had been *so much gaiety* in Moscow as that year (emphasis mine).[3]

Whatever the reasons, frivolity is most certainly a part of American culture. The United States has been described as a society addicted to fun: television sitcoms, sensational motion pictures, rock and rap music, recreational sex and drugs, spectator and participatory sports, Disneyland vacations. [4]

Invariably, companion characteristics to frivolity are the weakening of religion and the loss of traditional morality. More than just companion indicators, however, the decay of religion and morality are, in fact, the forerunners of a culture's lust for fun and games.

Don't Fence Us In

Robert H. Bork, in *Slouching Toward Gomorrah*, explains why this is so. The book has been called one of the 100 most significant books of the twentieth century. It offers what has been termed "a prophetic and unprecedented view of a culture in decline, a nation in such serious moral trouble that its very foundation is crumbling."[5] The book is, in publishing terms, a "blockbuster." In it Bork writes that during the earlier stages of U.S. life "men were kept from rootless hedonism . . . by religion, morality and law." Bork suggests that, in addition to these factors, the necessity for hard work, primarily physical, and the fear of want held frivolity in check. But, beginning in the late 1940s and on into the 1950s, these constraints were progressively undermined by rising affluence.*

---

* *Slouching Toward Gomorrah* cannot be too highly recommended as "must" reading for anyone who seeks to understand the current cultural scene in the United States. Scholarly, yet exceptionally readable, the book examines in detail all of the characteristics of American culture which Glubb cites as being typical of an empire's stage of collapse.

Hard physical work is inconsistent with hedonism; the new [sophisticated, technological] work is not. With the time and energy of so many individuals freed from the harder demands of work, the culture turned to consumerism and entertainment. Technology and its entrepreneurs supplied the demand with motion pictures, radio, television and videocassettes, all increasingly featuring sex and violence. Sensations must be steadily intensified if boredom is to be kept at bay.[6]

"There is no significant example in history, before our time, of a society successfully maintaining moral life without the aid of religion."—Will Durant

The cycle thus launched inevitably results in a steady erosion of traditional morality, an erosion that tends to grow exponentially. Again, Bork insightfully explains why:

A culture obsessed with technology will come to value personal convenience above all else, and ours does. [The result is] impatience with anything that interferes with personal convenience. Religion, morality and law do that, which accounts for the tendency of modern religion to eschew proscriptions and commandments . . . of morality to be relativized; and of law, particularly criminal law, to become soft and uncertain.[7]

Will Durant puts the weakening of religion in American life into an ominous light when he writes, "There is no significant example in history, before our time, of a society successfully maintaining moral life without the aid of religion."[8]

And yet, as Jim Black laments in *When Nations Die*, the modern code of the humanists who dominate American culture today "tells us that the Christian principles upon which this nation is founded are dangerous, destructive and divisive."[9] For example, the Supreme Court ruled in 1980 that the Ten Commandments could not be posted on the wall of a schoolroom (they feared the "establishment of a state-sponsored religion"), and the courts have for years consistently chipped away at religious freedom.

Nonviolent prolife activists have been fined and jailed on technicalities; street preachers have been silenced; churches prevented from expanding facilities; religious symbols and displays in public—such as crosses and Christmas creches—prohibited; any reference to Jesus Christ or even Christmas ruled out in public educational functions, including prayer at graduations or sporting events—the list goes on and on. Any reference to America's Christian heritage is systematically being expunged from history textbooks and curriculum—even from federal buildings, where possible.[10]

Bork writes that "large chunks of the moral life of the United States, [and] major features of its culture have disappeared altogether, and many more are in the process of extinction. These are being, or have already been, replaced by new modes of conduct, ways of thought and standards of morality that are unwelcome to many of us."[11]

Consequently, as Black accurately observes,

> Millions have seemingly lost their moral compass, and to fulfill their innate spiritual longings, they are turning to a witch's brew of New Age beliefs, paganism, environmental pantheism, humanistic egoism, and even devil worship.
>
> Deprived of faith in the one true God, men and women will worship anything, even foreign ideologies and destructive beliefs that will destroy society. The pagan beliefs and false ideologies of our day have robbed millions of people of the meaning and value of life. And the tortured humanistic philosophies of America's social reformers have

contributed to a deep inner sickness that is destroying the soul of the nation.[12]

And So We Coddle the Criminals

But while judges and lawyers throughout America continue to indicate by their actions the belief that Christianity and traditional values are dangerous threats to personal freedom, the United States is rapidly becoming one of the most dangerous nations in the world.

A horrendous rash of workplace murders and massacres coupled with a series of terrible shootings at public schools throughout the nation give evidence that something is seriously wrong. Once a model of peace, prosperity and responsible citizenship, typified by Andy Griffith's mythical Mayberry, the United States has become, in Black's words, "a nation in chaos . . . in the midst of an unprecedented crisis of law and order."

Bork cites the report, "The State of Violent Crime in America," by author Ben Wattenberg in his book *Values Matter Most*. While the violent crime rate went up sixfold from 1957 to 1993, the punishment expected by criminals for crimes of violence and burglary declined dramatically. Barely one criminal for every 100 violent crimes is imprisoned, and millions of convicted criminals with histories of violence—including the most violent repeat offenders—end up on probation and parole rather than behind bars.[13] *The Reader's Digest* monthly department, "That's Outrageous," which regularly describes horrendous miscarriages of justice, often resulting in murder or violence by repeat offenders, is an ongoing documentation of these tragic facts.

The violent crime rate actually showed a slight drop as the 1990s came to a close. But a United States Council on Crime report, as cited by Bork, warns, "Recent drops in serious crime are but the lull before the coming crime storm." He explains:

> The population of young males in the age groups that commit violent crime is about to increase rapidly, producing more violence than we know at present. It is also likely that the coming young felons will commit more serious crimes than today's juvenile offenders do. According to the report, the literature indicates that "each generation of crime-prone boys is several times more dangerous than the one before it, and that over 80 percent of the more serious and frequent offenders escape detection and arrest."[14]

Don't Give Me That Old-Fashioned Religion

The rise in immorality is also frightening. While the media and the courts oppose and vilify Christianity and traditional values, ethics—personal and business—are abandoned, criminals are given more rights than victims, illegitimacy and alternative sexual mores are increasingly approved, the justice system is routinely subverted, and the widespread sale and distribution of obscenity and pornography is protected. Meanwhile, the traditional family is under fierce attack by the elite of the culture.

Little wonder that Judge Bork says that "American popular culture is in a free fall, with the bottom not yet in sight. . . . The idea that men are naturally rational, moral creatures without the need for strong external restraints has been exploded by experience. There is an eager and growing market for depravity, and profitable industries devoted to supplying it."[15]

The evidences of decline are all around us.

Pornography in movies, videos, art (so-called), print and now, pervasively, on the Internet, is a multibillion-dollar-a-year industry. In Bork's words, "What America increasingly produces and distributes is now propaganda for every perversion and obscenity imaginable."[16] On the Internet, for example, graphic pornography of the vilest sort (according to a Lycos search engine, there are over 46,000 web sites on bestiality alone!) occupies the lion's share of all sites.

"There is an eager and growing market for depravity, and profitable industries devoted to supplying it."—Robert Bork

---

And yet, when the Senate Commerce Committee several years ago approved a proposal to impose criminal penalties on anyone who transmits on the Internet material that is "obscene, lewd, lascivious, filthy, or indecent," a firestorm of opposition immediately arose from a coalition of business and civil liberties groups. The coalition, which included the ACLU and Time Warner, wanted no restrictions whatever.[17]

The depth of the perversion is illustrated by the fact that there are literally hundreds of child pornography magazines being distributed across the nation, read by depraved people who fantasize about sexual acts with boys and girls. Father Bruce Ritter, founder of Covenant House in New York City, which seeks to piece together the lives of kids brutalized by the pornographers, writes, "Just once, try to look at a picture of a three-year-old in a sex act with an animal while an adult takes her photograph."[18]

Tragically, the greatest Internet demand is for pornography which is not readily available elsewhere—pedophilia, sadomasochism, eroticized bodily functions, fisting, sex acts with a variety of animals, nude children and incest.

The mind-boggling outpouring of such filth, like a constantly running moral sewer, has an incredibly degrading effect upon a culture. Pornography incites violence. Never in all of human history have a people had the widespread access to such filth as do the people of this culture and these times.

We Have to Be "Free"

Not surprisingly in such a climate, authority of any sort is mocked and rejected. A major factor in this growing challenge to authority is the influence of music. Jim Black, in discussing the fact that the most destructive forces in America today are those which are effectively transmitted to the middle class and become sociological patterns, maintains that music is one of the most powerful of these forces. He says,

> Much of today's rap music incites "cop killers," and death metal promotes violence, sexual and chemical abuse, satanism, hedonism, and utter self-destruction. Young adults and even small children who become fixated on MTV and VH-1 are indoctrinated with dangerous ideas about sex, violence, and flagrant disrespect for every form of authority.[19]

That such so-called music, described by writer Michael Bywater as "knuckle-dragging, sub-pidgin grunts and snarls, capable of fully expressing only the most pointless forms of violence and the most brutal forms of sex," should be allowed free reign in a culture is almost inconceivable. Vile lyrics, too filthy to reproduce here, in songs like "Horny," "Cop Killers" and "Big Man with a Gun" serve only to glorify perversity, violence, domination and rejection of authority. Yet these and similar degradations become best-sellers, impacting by the millions not just inner city youth, but white suburbanites and others.[20] Incredibly, these obscene assaults on decency and authority have become culturally acceptable, with the immoral "artists" popular, wealthy and part of the current crop of heroes.

Michael Jones, author of *Dionysis Rising: The Birth of Cultural Revolution Out of the Spirit of Music*, puts his finger on the effect nihilistic music has on a culture. The jacket blurb summarizes it:

> Jones reveals how major figures connected with modern music projected their own immorality into the field of music which has been the main vehicle of cultural revolution in the West. For the first time ever, a unified theory of music and cultural revolution links the works of Nietzsche, Schonberg, Jagger and others to show the connection between the demise of classical music and rise of rock 'n' roll.
>
> Beginning with Nietzsche's appropriation of Wagner's opera *Tristan and Isolde*, music became the instrument for cultural upheaval. What began at the barricades of Dresden in 1899 found its culmination at Woodstock and Altamont and the other Dionysian festivals of 1969.[21]

Most observers of the culture agree: the '60s were a watershed (though tragically not the culmination suggested above), which gave expression to a vast hatred for America by the radical youth of the era. That expression came in the form of the rejection of culture and morals, and in "filthy speech" language, sexual promiscuity, drug use, disdain for the military and for conventional success. The '60s radicals so completely revolted against the entire American culture that they believed the only legitimate response was its destruction.

They tried to destroy it—unsuccessfully, it seemed at the time. But without doubt, the seeds of America's demise were sown then. And rock music was the voice of the revolution, a voice that has risen to a deafening crescendo in the early days of a new millennium.

And the List Goes On

The tragic litany of America's cultural woes seems almost endless.

Disregard for human life, seen not only in the climate of violence, but more specifically in the acceptance of abortion, euthanasia and assisted suicide, tears at the very fabric of the nation. Illegitimacy is at epidemic levels, the increasing balkanization of the country bodes ill for the future, and beneath it all is the steady and increasingly rapid erosion of religion's influence.

Entire volumes could be written on each of the above indications of an empire in decline. Such a task is obviously beyond the scope of this book, so brief comments on these last few of Sir John's indicators of an empire's imminent collapse must suffice.

Because the family in America today, according to the Family Research Council, is undeniably weaker than at any point in our nation's history, children are no longer the treasure they were once believed to be. In reality, in an increasingly selfish society, many couples do not want to have children: they are viewed as an inconvenience and an interference in the pursuit of pleasure or career. Consequently the number of "DINK" couples (**d**ouble **i**ncome, **n**o **k**ids) grows. It is unnerving to recall a similar situation in Rome as that empire began to collapse. Children were then also viewed as an interference, and yet unbridled sexuality resulted in numerous pregnancies. So the common ways used to prevent unwanted children or to get rid of those who happened to be conceived or born were contraception, abortion and exposure (infanticide).

Need I remind you that there is a chilling parallel in modern-day America—widespread promotion and acceptance of a great variety of contraception methods; over 1.5 million abortions per year and, what many consider to be a form of infanticide—partial-birth abortion. Very closely related to all of this (termed "killing for convenience" by

Bork), are the horrors of assisted suicide and euthanasia, practices which were also part of the final days of Rome.

No Marriage License in Sight

Charles Murray, political scientist and author, identifies yet another indicator of moral collapse. He contends that "illegitimacy is the single most important social problem of our time—more important than crime, drugs, poverty, illiteracy, welfare, or homelessness because it drives everything else."[22] Murray shows how, when the black illegitimacy percentage (now approaching seventy percent) passed twenty-five percent, the black trendlines in crime, labor force dropout and illegitimacy all shot up rapidly.

Theorizing that twenty-five percent illegitimacy is a tipping point, Murray points with concern to the statistics which show that, as early as 1991, twenty-two percent of white births were illegitimate. While the majority of such births have been to white women below the poverty line, the growing tendency and cultural acceptance is for upper income women, as well, to become mothers without the benefit of marriage—all of this led by a rash of movie stars and feminists who shamelessly and brazenly glorify their out-of-wedlock motherhood.

If Murray's tipping point theory is correct, the white lower class is on the verge of becoming an underclass, with predictably dire results for society. He writes: "Either we reverse the current trends in illegitimacy—especially white illegitimacy—or America must, willy-nilly, become an unrecognizably authoritarian, socially segregated, centralized state."[23]

Divided We Fall

With tremendous insight, Bork writes:

Radical individualism, radical egalitarianism, omnipresent and omni-incompetent government, the politicization of the culture, and the battle for advantages through politics shatter a society into fragments of isolated individuals and angry groups. Social peace and cohesion decline as loneliness and alienation rise. Life in such a culture can come close to seeming intolerable.

A fragmented society, one in which a sense of community has disappeared, is necessarily a society with *low morale* (emphasis mine).[24]

At this point, it is profoundly unsettling to consider the words of historian Will Durant in *The Lessons of History,* written after he and his wife had completed their massive ten-volume, *The Story of Civilization.* In his summary of what he believed can be learned from history he wrote:

On one point all are agreed: civilizations begin, flourish, decline and disappear—or linger on as stagnant pools left by once life-giving streams. What are the causes . . . of decay?

Caught in the interval between one moral code and the next, an unmoored generation surrenders itself to luxury, corruption, and a restless disorder of family and morals, in all but a remnant clinging desperately to old restraints and ways.

. . . Theologies lose credence and receive an external conformity without influence upon conduct or hope. Life and ideals become increasingly secular . . . the moral code loses aura and force. *Few souls feel any longer that "it is beautiful and honorable to die for one's country."*

At the end of the process a decisive defeat in war may bring a final blow, or barbarian invasion from without may combine with barbarism welling up from within to bring a civilization to a close (emphasis mine).[25]

Charles Colson, in *Against the Night*, adds further insight. He comments on the fact that the loss of transcendent values among politicians, which has generated a disturbing apathy concerning the political process, is simply a reflection of that loss in the electorate. Observing that citizens who are unwilling to put the civic good above their own can't expect their leaders to do it for them, Colson asserts that radical individualism thus paves the way for the death of community.

He illustrates the way personal autonomy has been elevated above community good by citing a *Rolling Stones* survey in which forty percent of baby boomers said that there was absolutely no circumstance under which they would be willing to fight for their country. Colson then quotes sociologist Peter Berger as saying, "Unless people are prepared, if necessary, to die for [their nation], a society cannot long survive."[26]

Bork describes how a fragmented society with low morale "displays loss of nerve":

> [. . . it] means that it cannot summon the will to suppress public obscenity, punish crime, reform welfare, attach stigma to the bearing of illegitimate children, resist the demands of self-proclaimed victim groups for preferential treatment, or maintain standards of reason and scholarship. That is precisely and increasingly our situation today.[27]

"Unless people are prepared, if necessary, to die for [their nation], a society cannot long survive."—Peter Berger

---

In the light of the above, Durant's lessons from history appear to indicate that the American empire may be at "end-game" stage, even as shown in Sir John's symptoms of an empire's Age of Decline and Collapse.

Much More Could Be Said

A great deal more could be written in an effort to document the signs of potential collapse all about us—such as the decline in education, which Black describes as being "held in a virtual stranglehold by liberal teachers' unions."[28] He maintains that consequently many of America's public schools have become ghettoes of ignorance and violence; that they are fountains of political correctness and fiercely antagonistic to Christianity, while openly promoting New Age and other pagan religious philosophies. Many are proponents of liberal sex education—devoid of morality; sympathetic to homosexuality and aligned with the federal bureaucracy, even as, in the fallen empires of the past, the cultural elites always attached themselves to government. Much of the above would also apply to the universities and colleges of the nation.[29]

Black quotes former Secretary of Education William Bennett as saying that, if not remedied, what he calls the spiritual "acedia," or sloth, of American public education will lead to the death of the nation.[30]

Still More Distress

To the above could be added a much more comprehensive documentation of the extent to which traditional religious faith in America has dramatically declined. The disturbing state of the traditional American family could also be far more fully detailed, including the steady increase in the divorce rate, the dramatic rise in the number of cohabiting couples, the absentee father in millions of homes, with the corresponding burgeoning number of single parents, primarily women.

There has been only brief consideration given to the enormous advances made by militant homosexuals in their agenda of gaining complete cultural acceptance—including the legal right to marry, which family proponents such as Dr. James Dobson of Focus on the Family claim could signal, in effect, an end to traditional marriage. Perhaps the sodomist movement should have been given greater attention inasmuch as some students of history maintain that *no* culture has ever survived the widespread acceptance of homosexuality as an alternative lifestyle.[31]

Nor have we addressed the very serious issues of the incomprehensibly large debt of the United States government—reportedly in the multitrillions of dollars or the steadily growing power of government itself with all the dangers that holds. The esteemed nineteenth-century French statesman and author, Alexis de Tocqueville, an admirer of America, warned then that the drift toward centralization of government is the very essence of despotism. He observed that "the rise of the all-powerful state is the root of the waves of egoism, selfishness, and self-seeking that perennially overcome great societies at critical times in history."[32]

Each of these factors could easily merit a chapter or volume on its own. Nevertheless, we will do no more than mention them and move on to note an extremely perceptive insight concerning the basic cause of the precipitous decline in America's national character.

A Potent Duo

The root of our decline, Bork argues, is the rise of modern liberalism which stresses the dual forces of *radical egalitarianism* (the equality of outcomes rather than opportunities) and *radical individualism* (the drastic reduction of limits to personal gratification).[33]

Bork shows how these two forces, which would appear to be mutually exclusive in a society, actually function. Radical egalitarianism operates in the realm of society where superior achievement is possible and would be rewarded *except* for the enforcement of equality through measures such as quotas, affirmative action and the more extreme feminist demands.

Radical individualism is the demand of people who do not wish to be hindered in the pursuit of pleasure, and finds its expression primarily in the area of sexuality and the arts. Bork writes:

> Sometimes the impulses of radical individualism and radical egalitarianism cooperate. Both, for example, are antagonistic to society's traditional morality—the individualist because his pleasures can be maximized only by freedom from authority, the egalitarian because he resents any distinction among people or forms of behavior that suggests superiority in one or the other. When egalitarianism reinforces individualism, denying the possibility that one culture or moral view can be superior to another, the result is cultural and moral chaos, both prominent and destructive features of our time.[34]

"[T]he rise of the all-powerful state is the root of the waves of egoism, selfishness, and self-seeking that perennially overcome great societies at critical times in history."
—Alexis de Tocqueville

The effect of these two forces is so powerful, says Bork, because modern liberalism has enlisted the cultural elite who control the "institutions that manufacture, manipulate and disseminate ideas, attitudes and symbols."[35]

Included in these are universities, churches, the movie industry, the national press (print and electronic), some foundations and public interest groups, many politicians and "large sections of the judiciary, including, all too often, a majority of the Supreme Court." This syndrome of liberal perspective, according to Bork, is completely pervasive and "commands the heights of our culture." Resistance comes only from what appears to be increasingly smaller segments of society, while the individualistic component of liberalism incessantly presses against the limits set by a sense of decency and shame. The "envelope," as TV and movie producers frequently announce, is continually being pushed. And tragically, the demand for decadent pleasures is there—it is not being forced on an unwilling public.[36]

Bork points out why this is so serious.

> The fact that resistance to modern liberalism is weakening suggests that we are on the road to cultural disaster because, in their final stages, radical egalitarianism becomes tyranny and radical individualism descends into hedonism. Those translate into a modern version of [the Roman] bread and circuses. Government grows larger and more intrusive in order to direct the distribution of goods and services in an ever more equal fashion while people are coarsened and diverted, led to believe that their freedoms are increasing, by a great variety of entertainments featuring violence and sex.[37]

In this light, it is most interesting to note what the famous English scholar, Thomas Babbington Macaulay, wrote in 1861 to a friend in America. He penned, "Your republic will be fearfully plundered and laid waste by barbarians in the twentieth century as the Roman Empire was in the fifth, with this difference: that the Huns and Vandals will have been engendered within your own country, by your own institutions."[38]

Black, who quotes the above letter, comments that though Macaulay was an admirer of America and hoped for her prosperity, he feared the dangers of egalitarianism and liberalism, and sensed that liberty itself would one day become the very source of her self-destruction.

Not surprisingly, Bork concludes his comments on the moral breakdown in American culture with this statement: "Unless there is a vigorous counterattack, which must, I think, resort to legal as well as moral sanctions, the prospects are for a chaotic and unhappy society, followed, perhaps, by an authoritarian and unhappy society."[39]

The Observers Are Pessimistic

In view of what we've considered in this chapter, it isn't a surprise to read comments like the following, culled from the writings of several respected observers of the American scene.

> "To ignore [these] problems . . . is to ensure that we *shall* be destroyed, both from without and within, precisely like the empires of old."

> "We can see the indisputable image of national catastrophe on the horizon, and the crisis is greatly compounded by the destructive policies of the bureaucracy. Our nation is in a financial crisis and there is strong evidence that America's day of reckoning is not far away."

> "Though its influence may continue for some time, the 'American Century' has come to a premature end, and America's authority . . . is on a rapid downhill slide. What lies ahead is a time of troubles that will threaten the very foundations of the modern nation."

> "When I think of America, I think of affluence, decadence, overly high consumption and overly high expectations. The face of America . . . is the very image of decline."[40]

Will America Die?

I am not a prophet, nor the son of a prophet, so I cannot say what the future will be. There are, however, several observations which can be made in response to that question.

A feature of the prophetic Scriptures which has long been something of a conundrum to prophecy students may contain a significant hint. The conundrum has been the apparent absence of any clear reference to the United States in the biblical prophecies concerning the end times. Given the global dominance of America for the past century, this fact has puzzled prophecy buffs for decades. Some have attempted to find the U.S. as a protagonist in portions like Ezekiel's prophecy, which describes Russia's leadership of a confederacy that invades a regathered Israel. All such efforts are, in my opinion, a stretch at best.

Past empires, though maintaining the appearance of strength, have collapsed suddenly, rotted away internally by moral decay.

Maybe the explanation for America's absence in the prophetic record is a simple though disconcerting one. Maybe the empire which is the United States today will have collapsed, leaving (to quote Will Durant) "only stagnant pools where once there were life-giving streams."[41]

Improbable as it may seem to some, it is a scenario which is not beyond the realm of possibility. Past empires, though still maintaining the appearance of strength, have collapsed suddenly, becoming a shell of their former selves, rotted away internally by moral decay. In such cases, comparatively minor assaults from without have been enough to trigger the downfall.

Could it happen to the mighty U.S. empire? Has she come to the point at which attacks by "twenty-first-century barbarians" could prove fatal? A consideration of that possibility is next.

Endnotes

1. Edward Gibbon, as summarized and cited by Dr. Larry Poland in *How to Prepare for the Coming Persecution* (San Bernardino, CA: Here's Life Publishers, 1990), 76.

2. Charles Colson, *Against the Night* (Ann Arbor, MI: Vine Books, 1989), 57.

3. Leo Tolstoy, *War and Peace* (New York: Dutton Signet, 1976), 538.

4. Robert H. Bork, *Slouching Toward Gomorrah* (New York: Regan Books, 1996), 35.

5. Cover summary, *Slouching Toward Gomorrah* paperback edition, 1997.

6. Ibid., 9.

7. Ibid..

8. Will Durant, as quoted in James Black, *When Nations Die* (Wheaton, IL: Tyndale, 1994), 9.

9. Ibid.

10. For a detailed and extensive documentation of such restructuring, read *The Rewriting of American History,* one of several well-documented volumes revealing what is unquestionably a deliberate, concerted effort. (Available from Christian Publications, 1-800-233-4443.)

11. Bork, 12.

12. Black, 10.

13. Bork, 11.

14. Ibid., 10.

15. Ibid., 139.

16. Ibid., 140.

17. Ibid., 148.

18. Poland, 16.

19. Black, 109.

20. Bork, 124.

21. Michael Jones, *Dionysis Rising: The Birth of Cultural Revolution Out of the Spirit of Music* (San Francisco, CA: Ignatius Press, 1994), jacket copy.

22. Bork, 120.

23. Charles Murray, "The Coming White Underclass," *Wall Street Journal,* October 29, 1993, A14, as quoted by Bork, 158, 170.

24. Ibid., 171.

25. Will Durant, *The Lessons of History* (New York: Simon and Schuster, 1968), 92, 93.

26. Colson, 94-95.

27. Bork, 11.

28. Black, 78.

29. Bork, 12.

30. Black, 75, 85.

31. Bill Gothard, *Be Alert to Spiritual Danger* (Wheaton, IL: IBYC, 1980), 16-17.

32. Alexis de Tocqueville, *The Old Order and the French Revolution,* as quoted by Black in *When Nations Die*, 69.

33. Bork, jacket copy.

34. Ibid., 5.

35. Ibid., 11.

36. Ibid., 140-153.

37. Ibid., 11.

38. Thomas Babbington Macauly, as quoted by Black, 246.

39. Bork, 139.

40. Quotes from author Oswald Spengler, Hungarian historian John Lukacs, author Jim Black, journalist David Halbertson.

41. Durant, 8.

Chapter Ten

Twenty-First Century Barbarians

Between now and 2015, terrorist tactics
will become increasingly sophisticated
and designed to achieve mass casualties.

—CIA study *Global Trends, 2015*

Next [21st] century, America
will not exist in its current form.

—Deputy Secretary of State Strobe Talbott,
in a *New York Times* interview, September 27, 1999

Charles Colson in *Against the Night* provides a graphic description of Rome in the period shortly before the empire was dealt its death blow by invading barbarians. He writes:

The Romans believed their empire would last forever. Huge public buildings like the temple of Jupiter had stood from the beginning of the Republic, and the new Pantheon made even the lowliest citizen stop and stare. Marble pillars soaring straight in to the blue skies above the city embodied Rome's grandeur and greatness.

Vast libraries contained, it was said, all the books in the world: the learning of the past enshrined for the future. Roads radiating from the Golden Milepost in the Forum seemed destined to remain arteries of the thriving life of Roman civilization for ages to come, just as they had for centuries past.

No one could remember when Rome had not been the pinnacle of civilization. Its permanence seemed as certain as its greatness.

For the people themselves, life seemed not only secure but quite pleasant. Their basic needs met, they were free to pursue every conceivable form of pleasure; and in that pursuit, the comfortable Romans were deaf to the barbarian rumblings from the East. Even as the sparks of Rome's defeat were struck within the city by its own citizens, the invasions that would fan them to full flame were already beginning far away.[1]

Could it be that similar "barbarian" invasions—which may end the American Empire, already weakened by massive moral decay—are currently beginning far away? In the minds of many knowledgeable observers such may indeed be the case.

High Tech Terrorism

Some have suggested that international terrorists, armed with nuclear, chemical or biological weapons, may well prove to be the external barbarians of the 2000s so far as America is concerned. Unquestionably this is a distinct possibility. Already terrorism has touched the United States; there was grave concern at the turn of the millennium over the specter of terrorism when in the throes of Y2K fears a number of alleged terrorists were arrested.[2] The capability does exist of holding hostage an entire nation, even as powerful as America, with weapons of mass destruction smuggled into a major city like New York, Los Angeles or Washington, D.C.

International terrorists, armed with nuclear, chemical or biological weapons, may well prove to be the external barbarians of the 2000s.

A recent UPI release was disturbingly titled "U.S. Totally Unprepared for Bioterrorism." The article which followed described the grave potential danger posed by the combination of three factors: 1) the widespread technological capability of producing biological weapons of mass destruction, 2) the comparative ease of terrorists releasing these into heavily populated strategic areas and 3) the total inability of the United States to cope with such attacks.

"One hundred grams of anthrax properly dispersed downwind over Washington, D.C., for example, could kill between 150,000 and 3 million people in surrounding areas," Dr. Tara O'Toole, deputy director of the Johns Hopkins University Center for Civilian Biodefense Studies, said at the Center for Strategic and International Studies. "This would produce fear and panic all over the country as millions rush to doctors' offices to be checked out."

"Most frightening of all," O'Toole said, "is the ever faster pace of technological advance, which has made the know-how for creating, manufacturing and dispersing these agents of mass destruction widely available through open literature."

In addition to Russian stores of former Soviet bio-weapons of mass destruction, there are "a dozen countries, including all states named by the State Department as sponsors of terrorism, that have developed bio-warfare capability," according to O'Toole. "These weapons of mass destruction are potentially a way around U.S. military power," she said. "They could, for example, destroy overseas bases during a U.S. forward deployment" such as in Kosovo in 1999.

"This is the age of big biology, of unbelievable breakthroughs in the search for medical miracles," O'Toole explained. "But this goes hand in hand with the tools to make ever more virulent weapons."

No U.S. city has the capacity for a mass casualty situation, she said. Johns Hopkins, for example, only has five isolation wards for infectious diseases. Across the nation, "[h]ospitals are closing and emergency rooms are losing money," strained as they are by people without medical insurance. Most ERs resort to just-in-time staffing procedures, she said, "and very few nurses are hospital employees."

"In the case of an epidemic, security staffs and cafeteria employees would take off in droves, just as was the case in 1994 during the plague in Surat, India. The U.S. Public Health system is woefully understaffed, underfunded and not part of an integrated system. There are no beepers, computers or even fax machines in many places. Public health-wise we are simply not wired."

O'Toole also said that a recent exercise in Denver, code-named "TOPOFF," postulated the release of bubonic plague in a bioterrorist attack. "It was called off after four days because of the sheer exhaustion of the participants, and the 'epidemic' was still expanding," she said.

There is an urgent need for $3 billion a year over the next 10 years for research and development in bio-defense, said O'Toole. The U.S. Public Health system, she said, "must identify critical capacities to detect, track and contain [biological attack]."[3]

That such bioterrorism is already being tested in the U.S. is a theory being floated even by the CIA. In an article entitled "West Nile Virus Worse Than Believed," columnist John LeBoutillier quotes a CIA official as suggesting that the West Nile Virus may be a "test run" in which Iraq or other hostile powers want to see how such a biological agent might spread and how the U.S. public might react. Saddam Hussein's government is known to be focusing on the development of biological agents such as smallpox.[4]

Those Kings of the East

Or perhaps the Chinese communists, who have apparently obtained U.S. secrets that have enabled them to develop the capability of obliterating American cities with nuclear missiles, will issue an ultimatum that will completely enfeeble America. (It is interesting to note that China *is* quite apparently to be found in the end-time prophecies as the "kings from the East," capable of fielding an army of 200 million men [Revelation 9:16; 16:12]). The somewhat controversial *The Coming Conflict with China*, authored by Richard Bernstein and Ross H. Munro, two internationally known journalist/researchers, paints a well-documented and disturbing picture of "a turbulent period ahead."

A number of publications have attempted recently to document communist China's military threat to America. Foremost among these is *Red Dragon Rising* by Edward Timperlake and William C. Triplett II. Timperlake is a Naval Academy graduate who has served as a Marine Corps fighter pilot, a staffer in Congress and in the Defense Department, while Triplett is a former chief counsel to the Senate Foreign Relations Committee who has had more than thirty years experience as a China military analyst with the American intelligence community and as a China advisor to the Executive Office of the President and to the United States Senate. Their book is extremely well-documented with hundreds of source notes, including numerous declassified American intelligence documents.

The authors of *Red Dragon Rising* maintain that no regime poses a greater threat to global security today than communist China. They claim that "[a]rmed with the most modern weapons of mass destruction—some stolen from America's own defense labs—the communist Chinese government is a brutal, expansionist regime that has targeted America and its democratic allies around the world."

Red Dragon Rising details communist China's "fifty-year history of naked aggression, which has accounted for the deaths of millions"; her "continuing sale of weapons of mass destruction to the most brutal anti-American terrorist regimes"; and the Chinese army's murder of thousands of its own people during the June 1989 Tiananmen Square massacre. The book also reveals how communist spies stole vital national security secrets from the United States, including technology which now makes possible the targeting of American cities by Chinese nuclear missiles.

After quoting Jiang Zemin, president of the People's Republic of China, as saying, "I am aware of the fact the [U.S.] remains our chief enemy," the authors very disturbingly describe in documented detail what they believe to be China's most serious threat to America's security: cyberwarfare. They explain the threat by first listing a variety of disruptive results that would affect the nation if a competent and motivated hostile force was able to manipulate modern computer systems to create havoc. This could by done in a myriad of ways: by infiltrating and tainting food processing industries, disrupting airport radar systems, contaminating civic water supplies, shutting down electric power grids, jamming telephone and all electronic communications, looting bank accounts and attacking individual identities through the elimination of Social Security and Veterans Department records, driver's license numbers, bank accounts, credit card records and so on.

A Deliberate "Y2K Attack"?

All of these are examples of what is known as cyberwarfare—"information warfare," or more specifically, "offensive information warfare."[5] The authors ask:

> Is there something to this, or is it just the product of an overactive imagination? The concept of information warfare—and in particular, offensive information warfare—is perhaps America's most highly guarded military secret today. Most experts in the field believe that the United States is currently the world's information warfare leader. But the interconnected, highly technical nature of modern American society makes the United States "the most vulnerable country in the world" for this sort of warfare, according to the former director of the National Security Agency, our premier electronic warfare agency. *Every one* of the examples above has either been tried successfully or will be within the capability of hostile forces in a short period of time, and every one is of deep concern to the American government. The problem is real (emphasis in the original).
>
> More alarming, the Chinese People's Liberation Army has the world's largest information warfare program, after the United States.[6]

After an extensive description of some of the devastating effects that cyber attacks could have on the U.S. military, the authors write:

> Frightening as some of these possibilities may be, in our view the far greater risk to the United States involves the American economic, political, and social system which is essentially unprotected. As the Chinese People's Liberation Army notes, "America's economic system is extremely vulnerable to information attacks." The PLA even envisions imposing an "economic information blockade," noting that the more a country depends on imports "the greater the damage to the economy." The United States, a nation that imports well over 50 percent of its oil and gas, could be quite vulnerable.
>
> *In fact, it is our judgment that information warfare from the People's Republic of China is an unheralded national security threat to*

the United States and the rest of the democratic countries (emphasis in the original).[7]

The authors point out that the PLA is rapidly achieving the five capabilities of effective information warfare: signals intelligence, supercomputers, trained technical personnel, sophisticated weaponry and strategic planning. And though the People's Republic of China had none of the essential supercomputers at the beginning of 1996, altered U.S. export control regulations that year permitted their sale to China, with the result that 600 American supercomputers had been purchased by the People's Republic by the end of 1998![8]

"America's economic system is extremely vulnerable to information attacks."—Chinese People's Liberation Army, as quoted by Edward Timperlake and William Triplett

---

Other factors which support the thesis of *Red Dragon Rising* include the fact that, though the move was greatly opposed, operational control of the strategic Panama Canal was turned over to Hutchison Whampoa, a Hong Kong-based Chinese-controlled company in 1999, and that the same company completed construction in 2000 of the world's largest container port in Freeport, Bahamas—just sixty miles from Florida. The company's web site boasts that the location is "one of the most strategic ports in the world because Freeport is the closest offshore port on the east coast of the United States, at the crossroads of routes between Europe and the Americas and through the Panama Canal." U.S. officials, including Senate Majority Leader Trent Lott, have expressed concern over these developments, with Lott describing the Hong Kong firm as "an arm of the People's Liberation Army." In spite of the denial of any links between the company and the communist regime, records indicate that Chinese government and military leaders have shown an inordinate interest in the Freeport facility, with numerous visits.[9]

On June 20, 2000, the White House issued a warning that the United States was vulnerable to an "electronic Pearl Harbor." The Associated Press release indicated that

> The United States is very vulnerable to electronic attack from enemy countries unless government and private business band together to fight the threat, according to a senior White House advisor.
>
> "We're talking about an electronic Pearl Harbor," Richard Clarke, a special advisor to the President on counter-terrorism, told a conference on cybercrime. "We have the equivalent today of enemy aircraft flying over the target, day after day."[10]

> In a Reuters news dispatch from Baltimore on October 16, 2000, the head of the super-secret U.S. National Security Agency (NSA) said that cyberspace had become as important a potential battlefield as any other and held out the prospect of attacking there as well as defending. "Information is now in a place," Air Force Lt. Gen. Michael Hayden told a major computer security conference. "It is a place where we must ensure American security as surely as on sea, air and space."[11]

> In a November 15, 2000 front-page article entitled "China Eyes War vs. No. 1 Enemy," the *Washington Post* reported that, "Within the inner circles of Communist China, the possibility of waging war against the United States is coming to dominate the thinking of the leadership." A variety of Chinese government pronouncements were cited, all "routinely portraying the United States as Enemy No. 1."[12]

While much more evidence could be marshaled concerning the potential danger to the United States arising from the Chinese threat or that of bioterrorism, such documentation is beyond the scope of this book. The brief material presented above is primarily intended to show that the possibility of such "21st century barbarians" delivering a fatal blow to the United States "empire" is not an unrealistic or improbable one. The lengthy *Washington Post* article referred to above quoted Liu Jiangjia, one of the People's Liberation Army strategists, as stating bluntly, "War is not far from us now."

Concerns such as these are held by very knowledgeable people. Under the headline "CIA Has Dire Predictions for World," the *Washington Post* reported the December 31, 2000 release of a seventy-page CIA study entitled *Global Trends 2015*. The article indicated that

> [The] world is on the brink of a new era that may resemble the script of a James Bond film in which international affairs are increasingly determined by large and powerful organizations rather than governments.
>
> These could include alliances between some of the most powerful criminal groups such as the Mafia and Chinese triads. Such groups, according to the CIA, "will corrupt leaders of unstable, economically fragile or failing states, insinuate themselves into troubled banks and businesses, and co-operate with insurgent political movements to control substantial geographic areas."
>
> The agency adds: "Their income will come from narcotics trafficking; aliens smuggling; trafficking in women and children; smuggling toxic materials, hazardous wastes, illicit arms, military technologies, and other contraband; financial fraud; and racketeering."
>
> In particular the study notes the growing threat of biological and chemical weapons and "suitcase" nuclear devices against the United States. In addition, it expects states such as Iraq and Iran to develop long range missiles in the near future.
>
> Iran, it says, could be testing such weapons as early as 2001, and cruise missiles by 2004. Iraq could have missiles capable of hitting

America by 2015, with both nations developing nuclear, chemical and biological warheads.[13]

The report does not make for happy reading.

Most of the recent government intelligence, security and defense reports fall into the same category. For example, a December 2000 White House National Security Council report warned of information warfare or sneak electronic assaults on America from hostile governments, drug lords, criminal cartels or terrorist groups that could crash power grids, financial networks, transportation systems, telecommunications and other vital services.[14]

"[The] world is on the brink of a new era that may resemble the script of a James Bond film."—James Langton

And on February 7, 2001, CIA Director George Tenet told the Senate Select Committee on Intelligence that terrorism is an immediate danger to Americans. "Never in my experience has American intelligence had to deal with such a dynamic set of concerns affecting such a broad range of U.S. interests," Tenet said. "Never have we had to deal with such a high quotient of uncertainty." While terrorism was the CIA's top priority, Tenet indicated that conventional threats such as intercontinental nuclear ballistic missile threats to the continental U.S. by nations such as China, Russia, North Korea and even Iran and Iraq are also concerns.[15]

And as if concerns such as these were not enough, news of the accidental discovery by Australian scientists of "the Doomsday bug" adds to the potential dangers. The altered virus, which was developed quite inadvertently while researchers were attempting to create a contraceptive vaccine for mice as a pest control, is described as having the potential for making the ultimate terrorist weapon, since it runs amok, wiping out victims within days and is extremely resistant to vaccines.

New Scientist magazine, which reported the discovery, indicated that the incident highlights how easy it would be for someone with bioengineering knowledge to create a murderous virus for which there would be no cure or effective vaccine.[16]

Is All Mankind Threatened?

There are other potential scenarios, some of which we will consider in Part Five. But a larger question is raised in the minds of many. It may well be that not just the empire of America is in fatal decline, but perhaps even that of all of mankind.

Unthinkable? Maybe not.

Again, in his Introduction to *Slouching Toward Gomorrah,* Bork writes, "This is a book about American decline. Since American culture is a variant of the cultures of all Western industrialized democracies, it may even, inadvertently, *be a book about Western decline*" (emphasis mine). And, of course, the prophecies of the Apocalypse, which unquestionably describe the end of man's rule upon earth, have existed since the first century. Could their fulfillment be upon us?

The consideration of this larger question is the subject of Part Four, next.

Endnotes

1. Charles Colson, *Against the Night* (Ann Arbor, MI: Vine Books, 1989), 25-26.

2. Richard Clarke, U.S. national coordinator for infrastructure protection and counterterrorism, reported on December 26, 2000, that militant Islamic terrorists headed by Osama bin Laden had planned a spectacular three-country attack for Janu-

ary 3, 2000. The plan called for multiple bombings in the United States and Jordan, as well as the sinking of a U.S. destroyer in Yemen. "January 2000 could have started with thousands of Americans dead at six or seven locations around the world," Clarke said. "We came very close to having that happen." The attacks either failed or were thwarted by arrests. U.S. officials refused to comment on current potential threats, but noted a sharp increase in threat reports in late 2000 (*The Washington Post,* December 26, 2000, A1). Of course, the terrorist attack on the U.S. vessel *Cole* in October 2000 was widely reported.

3. United Press International, *Washington Times,* August 23, 2000, 1.

4. John LeBoutillier, "West Nile Virus Worse Than Believed," NewsMax.com, October 23, 2000.

5. Edward Timperlake and William C. Triplett, II, *Red Dragon Rising* (Washington, D.C.: Tegnery Publishing, Inc., 1999), 121-122.

6. Ibid., 123

7. Ibid., 125-126.

8. Ibid., 127-129.

9. Christopher Ruddy and Stephan Archer, "Chinese Company Completes World's Largest Port in Bahamas," NewsMax.com, January 19, 2000.

10. Mike Blanchard, "U.S. Vulnerable to an 'Electronic Pearl Harbor,' " *The Calgary Herald,* June 20, 2000, A5.

11. Jim Wolf, "U.S. Spy Chief: Cyberspace Is Potential Battlefield," *Baltimore Sun,* October 16, 2000, A1.

12. James Langton, "China Eyes War Against No. 1 Enemy," *The Washington Post,* November 15, 2000, A1.

13. James Langton, "CIA Has Dire Predictions for World," *The Washington Post,* December 31, 2000, A1.

14. Jim Wolf, "U.S. Draws Attention to Information Warfare Threat," Reuters, December 26, 2000.

15. Washington (UPI), February 8, 2001, posted on NewsMax.com Wires.

16. "Aussie Scientists Stumble Across the Doomsday Bug," *New Scientist,* Agence France-Presse, January 11, 2001, 1-2.

Is the Empire of
Man Striking Out?

The late Malcolm Muggeridge, renowned and inimitable British journalist, once expressed in his typically colorful fashion what many thoughtful observers of our culture are reluctantly considering as a possibility.

Muggeridge wrote: "Having educated himself into imbecility and polluted and drugged himself into stupefaction, [Western man] keeled over: a weary, battered, old Brontosaurus, and *became extinct*" (emphasis mine).

Could this be possible? Is the extinction of not only America or Western man but also of the entire human race something more than mere dramatic rhetoric? Has mankind arrived at a point in history at which weapons of mass destruction too horrible to contemplate, or environmental disaster or resource depletion or some other catastrophe will ring down the curtain on us all?

The futurists are divided on the issue. Some envision a wonderful future, full of incredible developments, powered by mind-boggling technological advances. Others utter dire predictions, foreseeing the end of civilization as we know it.

Who is right?

And where do the biblical prophecies fit into the picture?

Part Four is a consideration of these questions.

Welcome to the future!?

Chapter Eleven

The Futurists:
Gloomy and Otherwise

I believe that we do face a crisis in Western culture,
and that it represents the greatest threat to
civilization since the barbarians invaded Rome.

—Charles Colson in *Against the Night*

Every measure of material human welfare
in the United States and the world
has improved rather than deteriorated.

—Julian Simon in *The State of Humanity*

It is professor Julian Simon's personal mission to "tilt at the wind-mills" of today's doomsayers. In his book, *The State of Humanity*, Simon draws a bead on authors like Paul Ehrlich (*The Population*

Bomb and Extinction), the Paddock brothers (*Famine 1975*) and even President Carter's *Global Report 2000*. While debunking the predictions of these and others who "focus on problems and disregard contrary evidence," the major thrust of Simon's collection of essays by fifty different writers is that "as bad as it may seem, life has never been better." And the future is just going to be more of the same, but even rosier.[1]

Simon is only one of many who are extremely upbeat about the new millennium.

Francis Fukuyama, who, as an obscure political analyst wrote *The End of History and the Last Man* in 1989, achieved almost instantaneous celebrity status as a result. Ten years later, he saw evidence that "the Great Disruption [had] run its course and the process of renorming [had] already begun." Fukuyama's vision of the future, as outlined in *The Great Disruption: Human Nature and the Reconstruction of Social Order*, is an optimistic one. The grand questions have been answered, he contends, and there's nothing to do beyond the technocratic administration of society.[2]

Newsweek columnist, Anna Quindlen, predicts that "the future will be grand because our kids will be its keepers." She details why, believing that youth today are "more interesting, more confident, less hidebound and uptight, better educated, more creative [than were youth in her era], and in some essential fashion, unafraid."[3]

Reason magazine, in December 1999, published a list of "Rotten Books" of the last half of the twentieth century, tomes that had gotten the future "Way Wrong." In addition to *Ehrlich's Population Bomb*, the list included the Club of Rome's *Limits to Growth*, Thurow's *The Zero-Sum Society*, Galbraith's *The New Industrial State* and others— most of which overwhelmingly had the theme that the world as we know it is doomed. Now, in the *Reason* editor's view, because past doomsayers have been proven wrong, it follows that the future will be great in spite of ominous signs on the horizon.[4]

Lawrence F. Kaplan, executive editor of *The National Interest* in Washington, D.C., takes issue with those who predict the collapse of the West. In a major article entitled, "A World Shaped by the West," Kaplan argues that, though the processes of globalization, political disintegration and the ebb and flow of state power are real and very evident, the changes created will certainly "overwhelmingly accrue to [the benefit of America and her allies]."[5]

The roster of those who look to the future with happy anticipation could easily be multiplied.

But There's Another Viewpoint

While individuals such as those mentioned above gleefully expose past inaccurate predictions and look ahead with optimism, a great many others have cast a worried eye at the future, voicing grave concern. Some of these concerns were recorded in the last chapter relative to America.

"Man has lost the capacity to foresee and forestall. He will end by destroying the earth."—Albert Schweitzer

---

But during the waning years of the last century there were numerous other pessimistic voices raised concerning the future of the world—voices like that of Albert Schweitzer who lamented, "Man has lost the capacity to foresee and forestall. *He will end by destroying the earth.*" Or that of the late behaviorist B.F. Skinner of Harvard who declared at age seventy-eight, "A decade ago there was hope, but *today the world is fatally ill. . . .* It is a very depressing way to end one's life. . . . The argument that we have always solved our problems in the past and shall, therefore, solve [these we now face] is like reassuring a dying man by pointing out that he has always recovered from past illnesses" (emphasis mine).[6]

University of Western Ontario professor emeritus, Ian Hunter, writing in *The National Post*, titled his essay, "Decline and Fall All Over Again." Stating that a rereading of Gibbon's magisterial *Decline and Fall of the Roman Empire* startled him with its similarity to the contemporary scene, Hunter commented: "The most striking parallel, perhaps, is the abandonment of moral law—not just sexual morality but such elementary precepts as truth-telling, promise-keeping, respect for private property, honoring of elders and any sense of decorum, forbearance and restraint."[7]

Other parallels which Hunter identified include

- an increase in law as morals are degraded
- a decline in the quality of leaders and statesmanship
- rapacious taxation which, being deemed inadequate, is supplemented by gambling income
- the yielding in art, literature and music, first to license and then to depravity
- the dissipation of wealth in luxury and frivolity
- the assault on marriage and family—the twin pillars of social stability
- the loss of religious influence
- the decline in the quality of education.[8]

Little wonder that the implicit question in Hunter's article is whether we are seeing the foreshadowings of the kind of total collapse which came to Rome. The symptoms have been developing for some time. Charles Colson recalls that "as Winston Churchill lay dying, he reflected on conditions in the world he had so heroically helped to rescue from tyranny. 'There is no hope,' he sighed. 'There is no hope.' And with that despairing observation, the great leader died."[9]

Perhaps Churchill was so pessimistic because he knew what others did not then know about world conditions at the time of his passing. Regardless, if he believed there was no hope then, what about now? The world has unquestionably become a much more dangerous place than it was when Churchill died in 1965.

There was worldwide euphoria back in 1989-1990 when the Berlin Wall came down as the communist world-movement apparently collapsed. It was hoped that a new era of global peace would come to pass. However, the horrendous ethnic cleansings and wars since—in Africa, Bosnia, Indonesia, Russia and elsewhere—have quickly dispelled all such hope. In such a climate, David Gress, political historian at the Danish Institute of International Affairs, suggests that the West is self-destructing. In his book, *From Plato to NATO: The Idea of the West and Its Opponents*, Gress expresses doubt about the survival of the West because of the loss of the fundamental values on which it was based, "values corroded by extreme egalitarianism, bureaucratic rationalism, and the anti-Western multiculturalism of contemporary neo-liberalism."[10]

Not surprisingly, Pastor James Toews asks, "Are we really watching Western civilization in its death throes?" Writing in *Encounter #14*, Toews opines that we may well be—and suggests yet another possible indicator that the doomsayers could be right.

Historically, when faced with real calamity, humanity has often demonstrated an enormous capacity for self-indulgence. During the First World War, pre-revolutionary Russia was bankrupt in every way, and yet Moscow was a city of extravagant dissipation. Germany in the 1930s was facing staggering inflation, unemployment and despair, and yet Berlin was known for its numerous cabarets and nightclubs. The focus on pleasure-seeking in our time could well support the view that something is seriously wrong.[11]

Gress expresses doubt about the survival of the West because of the loss of the fundamental values on which it was based.

While acknowledging that our technological civilization rolls on like a well-oiled machine, giving it an air of indestructibility, David Ehrenfeld, in an article in *Tikkun* entitled "The Coming Collapse of the Age of Technology," maintains that no civilization can last forever. Without considering the many ecological and technological problems, which he claims are capable of "nudging civilization over the precipice," Ehrenfeld declares that "our technological globalization is nearing its apogee; the system is self-destructing." He lists a number of forces which he says will lead to the fall: misuse or loss of information, increasing complexity and centralized control, the unnecessary exhaustion of resources and the loss of higher inspiration.[12]

Is Oblivion on the Horizon?

The startling title and the stark cover graphics of the book grabbed my attention first. Then recognition of the author's name, a man whose writings I knew and appreciated, held it further. A subsequent perusal of its contents captivated and disturbed me. The book, *Hurtling Toward Oblivion: A Logical Argument for the End of the Age,* obviously does not contain a rosy-hued vision of mankind's future. But neither is it a wild-eyed, paranoic diatribe by an irrational doomsayer.

The author, Richard A. Swenson, is a physician and futurist. Following thirteen years on the faculty of the University of Wisconsin Medical School, Dr. Swenson currently researches and writes full-time about the intersection of culture, health, faith and the future. He is author of the best-seller, *Margin,* as well as a companion volume, *The Overload Syndrome,* and is in demand as a lecturer. He has spoken to a wide variety of audiences including career, professional and management groups, major church denominations, members of Congress and the Pentagon.

Why the lengthy introduction, you may wonder.

Simply because it is important to realize that the author of this book on "the future we might not have"—which we'll summarize shortly—is bona fide. He's not some far-out fanatic, but rather a thoughtful, well-educated professional. Consequently, because of his stature and status, his disturbing thesis deserves careful consideration.

In a nutshell, Swenson describes the realities that provide a logical argument for the end of our age, combining in his presentation the trends of social change, the nature of mankind and the rapid, irreversible advance of progress and technology.

The Level of Lethality

Swenson's logic begins with a factor he terms "profusion." By this he means that in a world addicted to progress the irreversible drive is always for more and better. Profusion can only increase, he argues, because to call a halt to progress—assuming it even could be done—would be to destroy the world economies. Besides, no one wants to turn back the clock to a less technological, more personally demanding age. Who would be willing to revert to a horse-and-buggy economy? Probably not even the Amish folk. Therefore, mankind is locked into profusion which is growing exponentially in the extreme.[*] Swenson maintains that the exponentiality of profusion exceeds that of most other exponential curves by several orders of magnitude.

With each new level of profusion, says Swenson, we have much new "positive," but unavoidably, because we are in a fallen world in which all people and things are inherently defective, we also have much new "negative." As an example, the Internet provides enormous positives in education, communication, research, marketing, commerce and more. But it also makes possible unbelievable negatives: addiction, hate group use, bomb-making instructions, hacker intrusion into government and business, vicious pornography and so on.

However, the positive which results from profusion is, in fact, growing much faster than the negative. Consequently there is general optimism that things are rapidly getting better in the world, an opinion which is accurate in many regards and, on the surface, reassuring. Julian Simon is right in *The State of Humanity*: "[E]very measure of material human welfare has improved."

Nevertheless, while the growth of positive is exponentially rapid, the corresponding growth of negative, though not as rapid, is also

---

[*] We remind ourselves that "exponentiality" is the term for the mathematical operation of raising a quantity to a power which represents the number of times a quantity is multiplied by itself. Obviously each time any quantity is thus multiplied the increase is magnified dramatically. For a very simplistic illustration of exponentiality, check out the children's riddle described near the end of this chapter.

alarming. There are myriads of negatives, virtually one for every positive. Part of an illustration Swenson uses is the amazing mobility which modern transportation technology makes possible. We can be anywhere in the nation—or the world—in a matter of hours. While that fact is positive, a negative is that such mobility has contributed to the spread of disease, particularly AIDS, and greatly increases the risk of global pandemics.

Dr. Swenson then points out that when the critical mass of negative reaches a certain level of lethality, it will prove fatal for the world system because no amount of positive can offset the negative when it reaches the threshold of lethality.

He gives a number of illustrations to show how one lethal negative can negate dozens of positives. For example, you receive a packet of ten letters. The wonderful news of a million-dollar inheritance and eight other extremely positive announcements in the first nine letters is completely negated by the lethal negative in the tenth letter which is from the Public Health Department: Tests prove you have AIDS as the result of an inadvertent needle prick.

Dr. Swenson then points out that when the critical mass of negative reaches a certain level of lethality, it will prove fatal for the world system.

Or consider the illustration of the fifty-year-old man who has a marvelous body which he diligently and wisely cares for, meticulously following all the guidelines for good health of which he is a perfect specimen. But one day he comes down with a fever, his condition rapidly worsens, and despite intensive therapy in ICU, he dies. Culture and blood work later reveal a virulent respiratory virus picked up while he was wilderness camping. All the positive of his healthy habits and wonderful body does not matter once the negative reaches a level of lethality.

Swenson then asks: "Is there such a thing as a threshold of lethality for the entire world system?"

His answer? "Of course."

Several scenarios present themselves for consideration: war (especially involving nuclear, biological and chemical weapons, the so-called weapons of mass destruction), disease and environmental catastrophe, to name but a few.[13] He writes:

> No matter how many benefits of progress the world system enjoys, and no matter how rapidly these benefits accumulate, once the negatives rise to the level of lethality, the viability of the entire globe will be threatened. . . . At that point, the entire system will be doomed, no matter how much positive has been compiled. It makes no difference if we have ten units of good, a thousand units or a trillion units. Lethality will still win.
>
> That such a potential threshold of lethality exists for the world system is undeniable. The only uncertainty comes in assessing how far into the future such a threshold lies, how long it will take for us to reach this threshold, and if there is anything that can be done to prevent us from colliding with it. But from a mathematical point of view, we are approaching it at a very rapid speed—and continuously accelerating.[14]

Finally, says Swenson, "we have no possible option but to continue in this fatal direction because of our total dependency on progress."[15] That, my friends, is profoundly logical and profoundly disturbing.

It is manifestly unfair to Dr. Swenson to attempt to condense into a few paragraphs the careful logic which he so painstakingly develops in the chapters of his thought-provoking book. A careful study of *Hur-*

tling Toward Oblivion itself is therefore strongly recommended to any who wish to consider the full argument. Hopefully, however, sufficient detail has been provided here to help the reader understand that the concept of a literal end to the empire of man is not at all unthinkable. On the contrary, it is an unquestionably logical probability!

But We Look So Powerful

Someone may well ask, "How could this possibly be, given the magnitude and sheer immensity of our technological civilization, the empire which man has created? It looks so indestructible."

I'm reminded of the words of John Ralston Saul, who wrote: "Nothing seems more permanent than a long-established government about to lose power, nothing more invincible than a grand army on the morning of its annihilation."[16]

The power of the exponential factor is illustrated in a French children's riddle which The Club of Rome once utilized as a parable of the potential danger facing our planet.

Imagine you own a piece of property on which lies a small lake. Near the shore is a variety of water lily with a most unusual characteristic—it doubles in size every day. You understand that if the lily is permitted to grow unchecked it will completely cover your lake in thirty days, blocking all light and oxygen, thus choking off every form of life in the water.

But you're busy, and besides, the lily pad seems small in comparison to the size of the lake. For weeks you ignore it, deciding to deal with it when it covers half of your lake.

On what day will that be? The twenty-ninth day, of course. But by then you will have only one day left in which to save your lake.[17]

Could it be that the empire of man may well be in the evening hours of its twenty-ninth day?

Where Is God in All This?

To this point our data has originated entirely from people—intelligent, visionary, articulate—but finite creatures nonetheless.

Now, it's time to examine what the prophetic Scriptures have to say about the future of the human race and planet earth. What does the divine revelation from an infinite and omniscient God who sees and knows the future tell us?

That's our consideration in Chapter 12.

Endnotes

1. Review by Stephen Goode in *Insight*, April 1, 1996, 17-19, as reported in *Current Thoughts and Trends*, June 1996, 28.

2. Robert Sibley review, *Alberta Report*, July 26, 1999, 49.

3. Anna Quindlen, "Now It's Time for Generation Next," *Newsweek*, January 1, 2000, 112.

4. Peter Foster, "Famous False Predictions of Doom," *Financial Post*, December 31, 1999, 5.

5. Lawrence F. Kaplan, "A World Shaped by the West," *The National Interest*, December 29, 1999, A18.

6. *Philadelphia Inquirer*, September 25, 1982, as quoted in *Storm Warning*, 292-293.

7. Ian Hunter, "Decline and Fall All Over Again," *The National Post*, December 30, 1999, B15.

8. Ibid.

9. As quoted by Charles Colson in *Kingdoms in Conflict* (Grand Rapids, MI: Zondervan, 1987), 369.

10. Robert Sibley, "Whence Freedom?" a review of *From Plato to NATO*, *Alberta Report*, September 27, 1999, 38.

11. James Toews, "The End of Sanity," *Encounter # 14*, July, 1999, 8.

12. David Ehrenfeld, "The Coming Collapse of the Age of Technology," *Tikkun*, January/February 1999, 33-38. David Ehrenfeld, in his *Tikkun* article describes another fearful potential scenario: the NASA launch of the Cassini space probe which carried an energy source of 72 pounds of plutonium 238, the most deadly substance in existence. Its path, after swinging around Venus in order to gain velocity, brought it to

within an alarming 312 miles of Earth. Ehrenfeld comments that "foolishness of this magnitude will contribute to the downfall of our civilization."

13. Richard Swenson, *Hurtling Toward Oblivion* (Colorado Springs, CO: Navigators Press, 1999), 18-28, 19-20.

14. Ibid., 98, 102-103.

15. Ibid., 103.

16. J.R. Saul, as cited by Sir John Glubb in *The Fate of Empires and Search for Survival* (Edinburgh: William Blackwood and Sons, Ltd., 1918), 32.

17. As quoted in William R. Goetz, *Apocalypse Next* (Camp Hill, PA: Horizon Books, 1999), 21.

Chapter Twelve

The Biblical Prophecies

*Let no one make the mistake of interpreting
as mere fiction or hyperbole the Revelation passages
describing the Four Horsemen of the Apocalypse.
We need to recognize the Word of God
for what it is: the Word of God.*

—Billy Graham in *Storm Warning*

The Bible is full of prophecy, i.e., the predictions of things to come. Much of biblical prophecy has already been fulfilled. But there's obviously more still to come. In my first book, *Apocalypse Next*, I attempted to give a brief overview of end-time events by asking my readers to visualize multiple mountain ranges. I wrote:

> Perhaps the way to [understand] the future would be to imagine a series of mountain ranges stretching to the horizon, with each range or peak representing a prophetic high point. Think of the prophets themselves as standing at various vantage points in relationship to these ranges—some farther off, some closer, others actually within some of

the nearer mountains—looking upon this series of "prophetic peaks" and describing what they see.

Before we identify those peaks, one thing needs to be said about the Bible, the world's all-time best-seller. It claims to be the inspired, infallible Word of God and, in spite of vicious attacks upon it over the centuries, it gives every evidence to the intellectually honest seeker of being just what it claims. (To present the evidence for the divine authorship and authenticity of the Bible is beyond the scope of this book. Besides, it has already been adequately done by many scholars far more qualified than this writer—notably, in a popular format, *The New Evidence that Demands a Verdict* by Josh McDowell.)

As we come now to our overview of the peaks of prophecy, we recognize that from our vantage point in time we must look both back and forward. Some events recorded in Scripture are already history. Remember, however, that at the time the prophecies were uttered they were all prophecy, i.e., "history written in advance."[1]

The biblical prophecies that have already been fulfilled include:

- the foretelling of the birth, life, death, resurrection and ascension of the Messiah, Jesus Christ
- the descent of the Holy Spirit and the birth of the Church
- Israel divided, conquered and dispersed among the nations
- Israel regathered into a national homeland
- the rise and fall of empires.[2]

"The Bible claims to be the inspired, infallible Word of God and gives every evidence to the intellectually honest seeker of being just what it claims."—from Apocalypse Next

---

All were declared in advance; all were fulfilled to the letter.

But what about the as-yet-unfulfilled prophecies, those peaks which are still in the future and which forecast the last period of human rule? We are about to check them out.

When world-renowned evangelist Billy Graham released his book, *Approaching Hoofbeats* in the mid-1980s, it became a blockbuster best-seller with a first printing of 800,000 copies, at the time the largest first run in publishing history.

Approaching Hoofbeats dealt with the four horsemen of the apocalypse described in the sixth chapter of Revelation, the last book of the Bible. In vivid imagery, Graham outlined the dangers of earth's final days and pointed out that the first horseman depicts counterfeit religion—secular, anti-God, anti-Christian belief systems. The second horseman symbolizes war; the third, famine and pestilence; and the fourth, the trauma of death and hell.

While Graham effectively showed in *Approaching Hoofbeats* and in his more recent *Storm Warnings* that the foreshadowing of the events symbolized by the four horsemen appear to be all about us, that portion of Revelation is only part of what the inspired prophetic writers had to say about earth's end game.

Chronologically, there is much more in store for planet earth. Here's how it appears from Scripture as I understand God's Word.

Warning: "Heavy Stuff"

The following material is not light reading. Though it is by no means exhaustive, there is an enormous amount of detailed and sobering information here. Providing even this limited degree of detail is essential, however, just to scratch the surface of what the Bible says about the future. Numerous scriptural references are included to provide documentation; the biblical texts themselves are not given. Each reader is strongly encouraged to check out those references in order to be personally convinced of the validity of the position presented.

Please note: While not every future event which will be listed is related directly to man's empire, each event is a part of the panorama and so must be included.

On Earth's Agenda

Event Number One—The Rapture

Millions around the world disappear as the Rapture of the Church occurs.* This event is the return of Christ to take all those who have been born again and made righteous by faith in Him, both those believers who have already died, and those who are alive when the rapture takes place (1 Thessalonians 4:14-18; 1 Corinthians 15:51-58; Titus 2:13). This resurrection of the saints at the time of the Rapture is called the "first resurrection" (Daniel 12:2; Revelation 20:5-6). (There will be another resurrection which we will consider later.)

Can you imagine what earthlings will say when millions of people are here one moment and gone the next? The Rapture will obviously create quite a stir! I can just see the headlines now: "Millions Mysteriously Missing" or "Chaotic Conditions Worldwide." One New Age explanation for the missing millions already being floated is that the raptured are folks who have been removed by the "Higher Powers" to

---

* I am aware that some students of prophecy believe that the Rapture occurs at a later point, during or following what is called The Great Tribulation, most of which will be described in the remainder of the agenda we will outline. While no eschatological position is without difficulty, and while I make no claim to superior insight, I have become personally convinced that the above is the most accurate explanation for the timing of the Rapture.

be "reprogrammed," because through their "bigoted religion" (read Christianity), they are apparently holding back mankind's quantum leap into earth's "New Age."

The Rapture will be followed in heaven by the Judgment Seat of Christ. There, the actions of believers will be judged and rewards for good and faithful service will be issued to the worthy (Romans 14:10-12; 1 Corinthians 3:10-15). To celebrate the occasion, the Marriage Supper of Christ (the Bridegroom) and the Church (all believers—His bride) will then take place (Revelation 19:6-10).

Can you imagine what earthlings will say when millions of people are here one moment and gone the next?

The removal of so many people (Christ's body, the Church) from the earth means that the Holy Spirit, the "restrainer of evil" through His indwelling presence in Christians (2 Thessalonians 2:1-10), is also removed in the sense that He dwells in the Church, the preserving force or "the salt of the earth," as believers are called (Matthew 5:13). (Obviously, as omnipresent God, the Holy Spirit is here in the same way He was during Old Testament times prior to the birth of the Church.)

Without the restraining influence of Spirit-indwelt people, evil will flourish as never before. If it seems bad now—and it is—the outburst of wickedness after the Rapture occurs will be nothing short of horrendous. But God is prepared. He has a backup crew in the wings—144,000 Jews, 12,000 from each of the twelve tribes of Israel—who will do His work until such time as His assignment for them is completed (Revelation 7:3-8). More about that in a moment. As well there will be the testimony of the two witnesses (11:3-13) and of an angel who proclaims the gospel to the entire world (14:6-7).

Event Number Two—The Invasion of Israel

After the believers are gone, Israel will be invaded by a confederacy of nations led by Russia (Ezekiel 36-39). To provide full documentation for that statement is not possible here. (It has been thoroughly presented in a number of books, including *Apocalypse Next* [Chapters 5-7].) Suffice it to say that conditions for the fulfillment of the above prophecy are ripening in spite of the fact that Russia's "evil empire" has apparently collapsed.

Event Number Three—The Antichrist Takes Over

The Scriptures clearly foretell the end-time appearance of a global ruler who will 1) eventually gain absolute political and military power, 2) ultimately claim that he is God and 3) demand worship on pain of death. (The title "Antichrist" indicates that he is an *instead of* Christ.) To grasp the full meaning, consider the following Scriptures, remembering that the term "beast" is used to describe the Antichrist (Daniel 7:24-27; 9:26-27; 11:36-39; 12:11; Matthew 24:15; 2 Thessalonians 2:1-12; Revelation 11:1-12; 13:1-18; 17:1-18; 19:17-21).

This diabolical counterfeit christ, energized and empowered by Satan and supported by a counterfeit of the Holy Spirit whom the Bible calls the False Prophet (13:11-17), will enter into a short-lived union with a one-world church of sorts (Revelation 17), a counterfeit of the true Church, the Bride of Christ. Initially the false church (manifesting the religion of what the Bible calls "Mystery Babylon") will exercise control. However, the egotistical and satanically inspired Antichrist will ultimately destroy its power in order to subsume all worship to himself (more about that later).

From our present vantage point near the inception of the twenty-first century, does such a scenario really sound so far-fetched? Many prophecy students believe that technologically, politically, economically and spiritually the stage is rapidly being set for the kind of total control depicted under this final dictatorship.

To this point the events we've considered are those which are preparatory to the momentous occurrences which will have direct bearing on the end of man's empire upon earth. We turn now to an examination of those events which specifically bear on empire.

Event Number Four—The Tribulation

The Tribulation, as the Bible calls it, refers to a period of seven years during which three sets of divine judgments from heaven begin to be poured out on the earth.

The Seal Judgments

During the first stage of the Tribulation Judgments, God will visit His wrath upon the Antichrist and all those left in the world who have rejected Christ. This stage is described in Revelation 6 as the Seal Judgments. There are seven of these, the first four being the famous "horsemen of the apocalypse."

The first seal when opened, reveals a white horse ridden by a bowman wearing a crown. He is believed to symbolize a militant counterfeit religion which allows no rivals, i.e., the religion of the Antichrist which ruthlessly squelches all opposition (6:2).

The second seal unleashes a red horse whose rider has the power, given by God, to take peace from the earth and to cause men to kill one another. This red horse, according to Scripture, represents pervasive and unprecedented war and bloodshed (6:3-4).

The third seal, a black horse, is symbolic of a terrible famine. During those days, it will take one day's wages to earn enough to purchase one day's food (6:5-6).

The fourth seal reveals a pale horse which symbolizes Death and Hell (Hades). The awesome judgment unleashed by its rider results in the death—by sword, famines, pestilence and wild beasts—of one-fourth of earth's population (6:7-8). This mind-boggling judgment will mean the destruction of at least 1.5 billion people! Such unprecedented carnage will make the loss of human life that occurred during the Bubonic Plague—the great global flu epidemic which killed 18 million, or World Wars I and II in which 61 million perished—look minuscule in comparison. It will literally seem like hell on earth.

The fifth seal reveals persecution which results in the martyrdom of many of those who have received Christ after the Rapture (6:9-11).[3]

The sixth seal brings incredible physical upheavals. A great earthquake will rock the planet. There is also the suggestion of enormous volcanic activity. The sun will be darkened, and the moon will turn blood red. Stars will fall to the earth—perhaps the feared asteroid collisions—resulting in a shaking of the whole earth and the parting of the heavens. This parting will give the world's inhabitants a glimpse of Christ upon His throne. Intense but temporary fear will grip mankind (6:12-17).

The seventh seal ushers in the second stage of Tribulation judgment. Seven trumpets are given to seven angels who each announce another woe upon the earth (8:1-2).

The Trumpet Judgments

Incredibly, the Trumpet Judgments are more severe than the Seal Judgments. They begin at the midpoint of the seven-year Tribulation period of God's wrath upon earth and overlap into the final stage.

The *first trumpet* blows, and hail and fire mixed with blood consume a third of earth's trees and all the green grass. One-third of the earth is literally burned (8:7).

The *second trumpet* sounds, and a burning meteorite falls into the sea and pollutes one-third of earth's oceans. A third of all living sea creatures perish, and a third of all shipping is destroyed (8:8-9).

The *third trumpet* brings pollution of one-third of earth's fresh water rivers and springs, and a blazing star named Wormwood falls upon earth. The resulting "bitter" waters cause many deaths (8:10-11).

The *fourth trumpet* announces increased darkness upon the earth. A third of the light of the sun, moon and stars is darkened, i.e., a third of both day and night is without light (8:12). (Some have speculated that this is caused by a thick cloud of pollution.) This judgment is followed by an angel crying out, "Woe! Woe! Woe to the inhabitants of the earth, because of the trumpet blasts about to be sounded. . ." (8:13).

The *fifth trumpet* blows, introducing a five-month plague of huge supranatural locusts (probably embodied demons). They come from the Abyss (Hell). Their commander is an evil angel named Abaddon, and their sting causes agony like that of a scorpion. But it does not bring death, only torture. Men will long for death but will be unable to die (9:1-12).

The *sixth trumpet* unleashes four "avenging" angels together with a 200-million-strong force of demonic cavalry to destroy another one-third of mankind. The description of this army is terrifying—fire, smoke, sulfur, scorpions with injury-inflicting tails, etc. (9:13-19). Incredibly, those who survive still refuse to repent of their wickedness and continue to worship demons and idols (9:20-21).

The blast of the *seventh trumpet* brings an announcement—accompanied by a violent storm, an earthquake and great hailstones—that the judgment of the dead and of those who destroy the earth is coming.

The devastation, death and destruction which the first two stages of God's wrath—the Seal and Trumpet Judgments—will bring is almost beyond comprehension. A minimum of 3 billion of earth's inhabitants will die; the environment will be unbelievably polluted and the destruction to the earth resulting from unprecedented natural disasters will be massive.

Meanwhile . . .

While these Seal and Trumpet Judgments are taking place, the Antichrist reveals his devilish character and diabolical goals, and begins his reign of terror.

First, he destroys the false church in order to demand worship of himself alone (17:16-17). In doing so, he breaks an agreement he made earlier with Israel during his rise to power. He now forbids worship in the Jewish temple and substitutes for it the worldwide worship of himself and his image which he and the False Prophet have set up in the reconstructed temple in Jerusalem. This worship is enforced through demanding that people receive the mark—666—which alone will permit buying and selling (Daniel 9:20-27; 11:31-39; Matthew 24:15; 2 Thessalonians 2:4; Revelation 13:1-18; 17:1-18.)

All Jews who refuse to worship the Antichrist are selected for extinction, but supernatural aid from God allows many to escape and be preserved in what some believe is the present-day wilderness of Edom (Daniel 11:32-35; Matthew 24:15-24; Revelation 12:1-17). Again, according to some, at this point God permits the martyrdom of the

144,000 sealed Jewish servants of God as suggested in Revelation 14:1-5, as well as the slaying of many believers from around the earth who refuse to take the mark (7:9-14; 13:15; 20:4-5).

There will also be the intriguing incident of the Two Witnesses, proclaimers of God's truth, whom the Antichrist hates with an unholy passion. However, he is unable to kill them until finally God permits their death. The Antichrist and other God-hating people will celebrate that event by leaving their bodies on display in the streets of Jerusalem to be gloated over by the whole world (through global TV and/or the Internet?).

However, after three and one-half days, God resurrects the Two Witnesses and they ascend visibly into heaven in full view of multitudes of onlookers (a television event of mammoth proportions?). This "miracle," coupled with severe earthquake activity, will strike fear into the hearts of all mankind (11:3-13). This ends the Seal and Trumpet Judgments.

The Bowl Judgments

We turn now to the final and worst judgment of the series of three—the seven Bowl Judgments. These are more intense than those in the Seal and Trumpet phases, if that is possible. The pouring out of the Bowl of God's wrath produces horrific consequences (see Revelation 16).

First, ugly and painful sores break out on all those who have the mark of Antichrist and who worship his image (16:2).

Second, the sea becomes like blood, causing every living thing in it to perish (16:3).

Third, all fresh water sources become "as blood," a direct judgment for man's shedding of the blood of the saints and prophets (16:4).

Fourth, scorching heat from the sun sears the earth, causing unrepentant humanity to blaspheme the name of God as the source of the plagues (16:8-9).

Fifth, the Antichrist's domain, the earth, is plunged into darkness, intensifying the agony of mankind. The earth's occupants continue to defiantly curse God (16:10-11).

Sixth, the Euphrates River dries up in preparation for the "Kings of the East" to march on Israel for the battle of Armageddon. This sixth judgment also unleashes a hoard of enticing spirits from the evil trinity of Satan, the Antichrist and the False Prophet. This will lure the armies of the world to gather in Israel for Armageddon, "the battle on the great day of God Almighty" (16:12-14).

Seventh, a mammoth earthquake, the most severe in history, causes the cities of the nations to collapse. Mountains and islands are displaced, and huge 100-pound hailstones fall from heaven. Humanity's response is the continued cursing of God (16:17-21).

Beyond Description

It is depressing in the extreme to contemplate the awesome events as described in these judgments. They assault the imagination and understanding with their scenarios of inconceivable devastation. And certainly, from our finite point of view, they defy explanation. Whether these judgments are the result of the direct fiats of an avenging Creator or the divine use of intensified natural causes, such as massive solar flares and asteroids, can only be speculated.

Whatever else they are and do, however, the Revelation judgments unquestionably spell the end of man's empire epitomized by the reign of earth's final dictator, the Antichrist. At least, when the final event— Armageddon—is enacted, they write *"finis."*

The Biblical Prophecies

Event Number Five—The Battle of Armageddon

Maddened by hatred for God and His judgments, inspired by Satan and his seducing spirits and deceived by "The Lie" that man is god, armies from all nations will gather in Israel to war against the Almighty.[**] In their rage, they will ravage Jerusalem and destroy two-thirds of Israel's population as they seek to vent their anger against God by killing His chosen people (Revelation 16:14-16; Zechariah 12:3; 14:1-2).

At this point, the heavens will open, and the Lord Jesus Christ will be revealed with His army of saints. He will wreak vengeance and judgment upon His enemies:

- There will be a 200-mile-long strip of carnage in the Valley of Megiddo and the Valley of Jehoshaphat. (Joel 3:12-16; Revelation 13:5-17; 14:20; l6:14-16; 19:11-15)
- The Antichrist and the False Prophet will be taken and thrown into a lake of fire. (19:20)
- Satan will be bound by Michael, the archangel, and cast into "the Abyss" for 1,000 years. (20:1-3)

All those individuals who survive the Tribulation will be judged on the basis of their response to the gospel which has been proclaimed by Christ's "brethren" (the 144,000 witnesses, as well as "the Two") and by the angel who announces the gospel to the entire world during the judgment period (Matthew 25:31-46; Revelation 14:6-7).

[**]For an in-depth consideration of how it is possible that mankind could presume to literally fight against God, as well as a biblical study of "The Lie," please see *Apocalypse Next*, pp. 267-295.

Those who have rejected God's offer of mercy will die when confronted by Christ's awesome holiness at the brightness of His appearance (2 Thessalonians 2:8). But those who have responded to the gospel message will, with the believing remnant of Israel, enter the Millennium (a 1,000-year period) to repopulate the earth and serve under Christ, the Messiah King, and His Bride, the Church, i.e., all those who by faith in Christ have been born again through the ages and around the world.

Event Number Six—The Millennium

Christ will establish His earthly headquarters in Jerusalem and will preside over a 1,000-year utopia called the Millennium. Free from death, sickness, the presence of Satan and the effects of sin, such as war and the curse upon creation, mankind will enjoy a virtual Garden-of-Eden existence (Psalm 2:6; Isaiah 9:6-7; 11:6-10; 42:3-4; 65:20-25; Jeremiah 3:17; Zechariah 14:16; Romans 8:21-23; Revelation 20:4-6).

Man's empire here upon planet earth is going to end, and a new eternal kingdom will arise.

At the end of this marvelously wonderful 1,000-year rule of Christ, Satan will be released, and there will be a final rebellion, incredible as it may seem. Those born during the Millennium, who have lived all their lives under the benevolent, but nonetheless inflexible rule of Christ (Psalm 2), will have their personal opportunity to choose whether or not they will voluntarily obey God. The Satan-inspired rebellion by those who reject God's authority will be instantly struck down by fire from heaven (Revelation 20:7-9), and Satan himself will then be cast forever into the lake of fire (20:10).

Event Number Seven—The Great White Throne Judgment

Next in the line of end-time events is the Great White Throne Judgment. All of the unredeemed from throughout history will be brought to the judgment bar of God for final sentencing. Because their names are not written in the Lamb's Book of Life, they will be consigned to the lake of fire for eternity (20:11-15).

At this point, a number of things happen in quick succession:

- The kingdom which God the Father once gave to His Son, Jesus Christ, is now given back to the Father. This confirms Christ's Kingship, a formal completion of the work assigned to Him by the Father (1 Corinthians 15:24-28).
- The present heaven and earth are then destroyed with fire (2 Peter 3:10-13). This old planet, the home of man's fall, the curse of sin and of Satan's rule, will be consumed by God's purifying fire.
- A new heaven and a new earth are created. This is the place without sin where God will dwell with his saints forever (2 Peter 3:13, Revelation 21:1–22:5)—the Garden of Eden revisited.
- Down to this new world will descend the "New Jerusalem." (There is some debate over whether the New Jerusalem is an actual city or a symbolic representation of the church in its perfected and eternal state. Either way, it is eternal and comes from heaven. Like the original Jerusalem, it will be the place where God lives with His people.) (Revelation 21:1-7; 22)[4]

And so will dawn the eternal ages.

The conclusion is inescapable: Man's empire here upon planet earth *is* going to end, and a new eternal kingdom will arise. In other words, "Exit the Empire of Man; enter the Kingdom of God."

Summary

The question arises: *When* will the curtain ring down on man's empire?

Perhaps you have noticed what appears to be the fulfillment, before our very eyes, of a number of the end-time prophecies.

Could it be that we are living at the end of the age? If so, what should our response be?

That's a vital question. We'll endeavor to respond in Part Five.

Endnotes

1. William R. Goetz, *Apocalypse Next* (Camp Hill, PA: Horizon Books, 1999), 60, 61.

2. For detail, see *Apocalypse Next*, 61-71.

3. People will be born again during the Tribulation through the evangelism of three groups or individuals: the 144,000 Jewish "servants of God," sealed to do His work; the Two Witnesses of Revelation 11 and the angel described in Revelation 14:6-7 who preaches the gospel to the entire world.

As I understand Scripture, this conversion of people during the Tribulation is the only plausible explanation for how the earth's population, which is decimated during the Tribulation, can be restored in the Millennium. It is also a strong argument for the Pre-Tribulation Rapture view, for these reasons: If all believers are raptured at the end of the Tribulation and then immediately return with Christ in His Revelation, there will be no persons capable of procreation left upon earth. (Jesus said that in our heavenly state we will neither marry nor be given in marriage, Matthew 22:30, so as raptured beings we will obviously not procreate). Therefore, only if there are converted righteous human beings upon earth after the Rapture will there be people capable of replenishing earth's population.

I believe, however, that only those who have not previously heard the gospel will be able to come to Christ for salvation. According to Second Thessalonians 2:10, any who have heard and chosen to reject the good news before the Rapture will be sent a strong

The Biblical Prophecies

delusion by God so that they will believe "The Lie." There are many instances throughout Scripture which show how God confirms a decision to reject Him made previously by an individual. Pharaoh is one notable example (Exodus chapters 7 through 11).

4. *Quest Study Bible* (Grand Rapids, MI, Zondervan Publishing House, 1994), 1732.

PART

How Then Shall We Live?

So what are we to do? How are we to live?

If it is possible that we may be living in the final stages of mankind's history on earth, what course of action should we pursue?

Do we forget about long-range planning for career, future Christian service, our children's education or retirement? Do we forego investments, health care, home improvements and just live for today?

Actions such as these would be the equivalent of what unfortunately has happened on several occasions in the past. More than once, people—convinced of the imminent end of things—have sold everything, donned white robes and climbed a mountain to await Christ's return and the culmination of human affairs. Other sometimes bizarre methods of copping out of normal life in preparation for earth's assumed climax have often occurred, occasionally accompanied by prominent announcements in the major newspapers of the world.

Numerous "doomsday" cults, focusing on the dawn of the new millennium, further attracted media attention at the turn of the century.

Derision, when the anticipated arrival of the Lord or the end of the world did not occur, and subsequent disrepute for the cause of Christ have been the result of such behavior.

There is a better way.

And, as in every aspect of human life, that better way is spelled out in the pages of Scripture.

Let's take a look.

Chapter Thirteen

Lifestyles of the Wise
and the Unwise

The Christian faith is not just a theory,
not just a system, not just a framework. It is an
all-consuming way of life, robustly applicable
to every minute of every day of the rest of your life.

—Joel Belz, editor of *WORLD* magazine,
in a review of *How Now Shall We Live?* by Charles Colson

In one sense, I feel sorry for Jim.[*] Approaching retirement time, he is facing a somewhat bleak future. A sincere but, in my judgment, somewhat misguided Christian, Jim is convinced that the return of Christ for His Church will occur before he reaches old age. As a result,

---

[*] Name and exact circumstances altered to avoid embarrassment to the individual involved.

he has made little or no preparation for his sunset years other than what has been required of him by the government.

Now, in the natural course of events, he will have very little by way of financial resources on which to survive during his retirement. I know Jim. He is a godly man who has a strong faith in the Lord, and I firmly believe that God will care for His child. I admire and applaud his faith even as I also approve of his longing for and anticipation of an imminent Rapture.

But I feel sorry for Jim. He has apparently not understood the need for a biblically based balance between sensible preparation for the future and an expectancy of the Rapture at any moment. In effect he has opted out of the world. Thus, Jim differs only in degree from those who have on various occasions in the past sold or given everything away in anticipation of Christ's momentary return.

My friend's approach is somewhat typical of one of the several attitudes which can be and are adopted in light of the times in which we find ourselves. Let's consider the options.

Optimistic or Pessimistic?

There are basically three different kinds of response to our culture's danger signals.

One is to optimistically ignore them. A second is to react to them fatalistically, while a third is to adopt one of several pro-active positions.

The optimist chooses to dismiss or downplay the warnings, opting to live as though things will continue as they have always been. The optimist bends every effort to achieve for himself the best possible life now and in his foreseeable future.

The fatalist concludes that since prophecy is "history in advance" and thus cannot be altered, he can't affect its outcome. Or, quite apart from prophecy, he believes that since it appears that mankind is inevitably "hurtling on an irreversible one-way trip toward oblivion," nothing can be done by him personally to alter such realities. He therefore decides he should, as either a stoic or an epicurean, live for the moment since "tomorrow he dies."

The pro-activist adopts one of four lifestyle options: reclusivism, reconstructionism, restorationalism or revivalism, with the last two being quite similar. Let's define these lifestyles and consider their relative flaws and merits.

The Reclusivist

A reclusivist may behave like my friend Jim. Usually deeply sincere and fully convinced that end-time events, including societal collapse, are at hand, the reclusivist withdraws from legitimate personal or family responsibilities and/or from any effort to be salt and light in a darkening society.

Since the reclusivist believes that there won't be a future, his lifestyle takes the form of foregoing long-term preparation for the future. Consequently, reclusivists have sometimes failed to make proper career preparations, obtain an education or provide for family. There have even been instances of leaders in churches needing additional facilities shamelessly recommending unwise or excessive borrowing, arguing that since the Lord is coming soon the loan will not have to be repaid!

In extreme cases, some reclusivists have disposed of material possessions, donned white robes (figuratively or literally) and ascended some mountain to await the Rapture. A dramatic example of a non-Christian group taking a similar approach to its ultimate extreme occurred several years ago when the Heaven's Gate UFO cult committed mass suicide in their attempt to move to a "higher level of existence" by simply escaping a doomed world.

One of the net effects of taking a reclusive attitude, as already suggested, is to give up on society. Its evils are too many and too great; its doom is sure, and the time is short; so the logical thing to do is to opt out of any effort to have an effect on culture. Simply prepare yourself and your family for whatever is to come, sit tight and wait.

Admittedly, this type of reaction is comparatively rare, thankfully so. Such a lifestyle is most certainly not proper for a Christian, as will shortly become apparent.

There are numerous instances throughout history when God has withheld or delayed judgment.

The reclusivist response to the apparent imminent collapse of our culture and to biblical prophecy raises a question which Billy Graham addresses in *Storm Warning*. He says,

> As I review various commentaries on the Book of Revelation, I keep coming back to one basic question: Are the judgments that John foresees inevitable? Will they definitely happen, or can they somehow be delayed or even completely averted? In other words, are they conditional so that they may be avoided by repentance or faith, or are they unconditional and will happen no matter what?[1]

Dr. Graham acknowledges that the question is a difficult one and suggests that the answer is both! Judgment is certain. The Bible makes it perfectly clear that "[God] has set a day when he will judge the world with justice by the man he has appointed" (Acts 17:31).

But he also points out that there are numerous instances throughout history when God has withheld or delayed judgment as a result of the repentance and/or faith of people. Consequently,

> [We] must not feel that we are to sit back and do nothing to fight evil just because some day the four horsemen will ride with full and final force upon the earth. Yes, God's final judgment is inevitable, but He alone knows when it will come, and until that time . . . we are to act in such a way that God may be pleased to allow our world [more] time to hear His Word and turn to Him.[2]

There's no such action by the reclusivist, however.

The Reconstructionist

On the other hand, reconstruction theology, made famous by Gary De Mar, Greg Bahnsen, Gary North, his father-in-law, R.J. Rushdoony, author of *The Institutes of Biblical Law*, and others, seeks to recapture society and build an Old-Testament-era biblical order in which certain sinners, such as adulterers and homosexual men, would be severely punished, even executed, preferably by stoning.[3] The movement is quite extensive, with hundreds of books and newsletters, frequent conferences and a strong Internet presence.

A major theme among reconstructionists is the "glorious goal of worldwide [Christian] conquest!" One such writer declares: "We are to pull down the ungodly strongholds of this world, and we are to erect godly institutions in their place. . . ." Reconstructionist David Chilton maintains that "Christianity is destined to take over all the kingdoms of the earth . . . ," while Gary North writes that "God wants Christians to control the earth on His behalf. . . . [We] want to see a Biblical reconstruction of the United States, so that it can serve as an example to be followed all over the world."[4]

North, who gained notoriety through his web site in the final months of the twentieth century as a Y2K "expert," has long predicted social disorder and collapse through one threat or another, such as nuclear war, AIDS or Y2K. Society's collapse, which he inaccurately predicted would be caused by the millennium bug, fits in with his theology and his hope that out of the ashes of the present world system the kingdom of God will be brought in—by reconstructionists. Only after Draconian biblical law has been thus imposed for a thousand years will Christ return.

Were reconstructionists to succeed in their desire to have the Law of God, as codified in the Old Testament instituted as the law of the United States—and ultimately every other nation on earth—blasphemy would be a criminal offense, homosexuality a capital offense and slavery (in some form) reinstituted—all before the return of Christ to earth could occur.[5]

Obviously, in this postmillennial view, the book of Revelation is not to be taken literally but rather spiritualized. The Great Commission is reinterpreted to mean that believers work through political means to establish righteousness on earth. And though reconstructionists were hopeful in the 1980s when political conservatives posted gains in the U.S., recent trends have made their position increasingly difficult to support practically as well as theologically.

The bottom line is that reconstructionism is thoroughly unbiblical[6] and is obviously not the kind of response to the potential collapse of our culture which a Christian should adopt anymore than is the response of reclusivism.

The Restorationist

A restorationist lifestyle is different than a reconstructionist one. Perhaps the most extensive and recent declaration of the difference is found in Charles Colson's latest book *How Now Shall We Live?* In an interview about the then-forthcoming book in his own Prison Fellowship's *Jubilee* magazine (summer 1999), Colson was asked about triumphalism.

> *Jubilee*: You and [co-author] Nancy Pearcey write that the goal [of your book] is "to equip believers to be nothing less than God's agents in building a new Christian culture." How would you respond to someone who might accuse you of promoting a Christian utopianism?
>
> *Colson*: We're not touting utopianism, because we don't believe that the kingdom of God is going to be brought in by human means—not even by all the best efforts of Christians to bring Christian truth to society and to influence culture. . . . We're not talking about Christian triumphalism. We are talking about bringing Christian truth to bear on all areas of life. . . . We're saying this is a holding action until Christ returns.[7]

In the interview, Colson emphasized the fact that it is not enough for a Christian simply to be saved and assured of heaven, living happily as a believer, with one's family blessed by the application of Christian principles. The biblical mandate is to be salt and light which, in the current post-Christian culture, means to truly understand the biblical Christian worldview, be able to defend the faith and to live so as to bring Christian truth back into a dominant role in the culture. He reiterated, however, that

> I'm not talking about taking over society or violating the separation between church and state . . . [but about] an opportunity for the Church to retake the structures of our society, not by a heavy-handed moralistic crusade, not by political action, but by Christians understanding their faith and living their faith, their minds transformed.[8]

Having a Christian worldview which one understands and can articulate is vital, said Colson, because

[f]irst, every action you take is the result of [your] worldview. . . . What you believe to be true is going to influence how you behave.

Second, a worldview becomes crucially important because you need a context in which to evangelize. . . . You need to understand the culture [because] if you say Jesus is the answer and people don't know the question, you haven't accomplished anything.

Third, understanding the collision of worldviews becomes imperative if you're going to defend the faith and influence the culture. You have to know what the culture believes and why it is false, and what you believe and why it is true.[9]

Having a Christian worldview which one understands and can articulate is vital.

So, the restorationist is aware of the awful decadence of the culture, understands that the Christian worldview is the only one that is rationally sustainable, is able to articulate that worldview and genuinely seeks to be salt and light in a decaying and darkening world. This kind of lifestyle is similar to that of the revivalist.

The Revivalist

The major difference between the restorationist and the revivalist is that the latter tends to focus more directly on the need for the individual and the Church to be in right relationship to God, with the impact on culture being an outgrowth of personal revival.

Revivalism is not to be confused with "revivals," a term frequently used to describe a series of evangelistic meetings. Nor is it an upsurge of religious enthusiasm or a set of deeper-life conferences, though all of these may be beneficial. "Revival" is basically a deep and ongoing personal relationship with God resulting in a righteous effect on the community.

Dr. Ted Rendall, in *Fire in the Church*, defines "revival" using the biblical description given in First Samuel.

> First, revival means a fresh communication of God's Word. Though Israel had the law of God, until Samuel, the prophet, communicated it in living, contemporary, authoritative tones, its impact was rare. [Revival means God's voice is effectively heard.] (1 Samuel 3:1, 20).
>
> Second, revival involves a fresh consciousness of God's presence with His people. In revival God manifests Himself as the living God. . . . It is the Lord Himself who engages the affections and attention of His people. [Revival means God is central, worshiped and adored.] (I Samuel 3:21).
>
> Third, revival includes a fresh commitment to God's holy and just requirements. [Revival means full and complete obedience to what God demands of His people.] (I Samuel 7:4).[10]

"Revival" is basically a deep and ongoing personal relationship with God resulting in a righteous effect on the community.

Hearing God's voice, sensing God's presence and obeying God's Word—this is the measure of personal revival. It's another way of expressing what God said He wanted from His people: "Hear O Israel. . . . Love the LORD your God with all your heart and with all your soul and with all your strength. . . . Be sure to keep the commands of the LORD your God" (Deuteronomy 6:4-5, 17).

The revivalist lifestyle has been described as "the normal Christian life." It begins with the experience of the new birth through faith in the

Lord Jesus Christ and continues to be energized by the power of the Holy Spirit through fellowship with God and love for Him in consistent obedience to His Word and His will.

We will take a brief look at such a life in more detail in Chapter 13.

Endnotes

1. Billy Graham, *Storm Warning* (Dallas, TX: Word, 1992), 139.

2. Ibid., 141. Can an empire, deep into its Age of Collapse, have its life extended by a revival of spiritual life and morality? This important question arose in the minds of thoughtful individuals in the wake of the 2001 transition in the U.S. presidential administration. It is fair to say that the Clinton administration—which he declared would be "the most ethical in U.S. history"—turned out to be the most unethical, an assessment which only rabid partisans would dispute.

In contrast, President Bush—who campaigned on the promise to restore dignity and ethical behavior to the Oval Office—appears to be determined to do just that insofar as he is able. Is such a change in the character of an empire's leadership enough to alter the empire's future?

To explore such an intriguing question fully is beyond the scope of this volume. An adequate examination would demand a book of its own. However, several brief observations are in order. While no dogmatic conclusions can be drawn, there is nevertheless evidence from the pages of both biblical and secular history which suggests that spiritual revival can delay the death of an empire or a nation.

Take, for instance, the chosen people who, following the high point of Israel's nationhood under Solomon, were divided into two kingdoms in 930 B.C.—the ten northern tribes of Israel and the two southern tribes of Judah. The scriptural history recorded in Second Kings and Second Chronicles reveals that Israel had twenty kings, all of whom are described as evil (although two, Jehu and Jehoahaz, did partially obey the Lord). The northern kingdom lasted only 208 years, until 722 B.C., when its peoples were taken into Assyrian captivity, from which there never was a complete return.

While Judah also had twenty kings, the Bible, in contrast, describes eight of them as good or godly rulers who lived righteously, suppressed evil and led the nation into obedience to and proper worship of Jehovah. This kingdom survived for 344 years until the Babylonians conquered it. Even then, after seventy years of captivity, Judah was restored. The nation continued to exist under a succession of oppressors until 70 A.D. when the Roman general Titus finally uprooted and dispersed the Jews throughout the world.

Lifestyles of the Wise and the Unwise

The bottom line is that Judah continued as a nation in some form for 1,000 years, while Israel lasted only a little more than 200. Apparently, the influence of even a few godly leaders who sparked revival in Judah's history had an effect.

The book of Jonah and the history of the Assyrian Empire appear to support such a conclusion. In approximately 785 B.C. the Hebrew prophet, Jonah, was directed by the Lord to go and pronounce divine judgment against Nineveh, the capital of the evil Assyrian Empire. When he finally reluctantly obeyed, the Ninevites wholeheartedly repented. Then, just as Jonah had feared—since he was hoping for God's vengeance, not mercy, upon the Assyrian enemy—Jehovah withheld His judgment. The Assyrian Empire was spared, in effect, by a genuine revival.

And what about the British Empire? It, too, in the opinion of many, was prolonged and developed by the spiritual revival under John and Charles Wesley (1730-1791). The prospects for England and the Empire when the Wesleys came on the scene were dark indeed. Morality was at an all-time low. Spiritual life within the church was at an even lower ebb. France was heading for revolution, while during the Wesleys' lifetime, the American Revolution dealt the Empire a severe blow.

The impact of Wesley's ministry was powerful. Historian Will Durant, no proponent of Christianity, offers this assessment of the effects of Wesley's Methodism in *The Age of Voltaire*, Part IX of *The Story of Civilization:*

> What were the results of Methodist preaching? . . . In the great conflict between faith and reason it placed all its hopes on faith; it put no trust in the progress of knowledge and science; it ignored or scorned the Enlightenment that was setting France on fire. . . . If we judge greatness by influence, [Wesley] was, barring Pitt, the greatest Englishman of his times. (Will and Ariel Durant, *The Age of Voltaire,* Part IX of *The Story of Civilization* [New York: Simon and Schuster, 1965], 137)

Jeff Ziegler and Jay Rogers, in "Revival and Spiritual Awakening" in *The Forerunner,* write:

> Historians testify that it was [Wesley's] Methodists who provided the moral ballast that kept England from sliding into the same bloody tragedy which was experienced just a short distance away in the French Revolution of 1789. (Jeff Ziegler and Jay Rogers, "Revival and Spiritual Awakening," *The Forerunner,* November/December 1991, 3)

Wesley has been called one of the greatest Englishmen of his time, powerful, influential, even awe-inspiring according to various historians. "By the end of his life he had trained 750 preachers in England, and through his student Francis Asbury, 350 in America. At his death there were 79,968 Methodists in England and 57,612 in America" (*The Forerunner*, November-December 1991, 3).

Andrew Blackwood, in a chapter entitled "Lessons for Today" in *Revivals: Their Laws and Leaders,* adds to the evidence: "No student of church history can ignore or minimize the moral betterment that followed the work of Luther in Middle Europe, of Calvin in Geneva, of Knox in Scotland . . . and of Wesley in England. As a rule, then as now, moral betterment came as a by-product of revival and evangelism, both of them Biblical and doctrinal" (James Burns, *Revivals: Their Laws and Leaders,* [Grand Rapids, MI: Baker Book House, 1960], 339).

The crucial question must be asked: Could the American Empire, so extensively manifesting the characteristics of the Age of Collapse, be spared and its life prolonged by a genuine revival? The testimony of Scripture and history would appear to answer "Yes!"

Will such a revival come?

The answer to that all-important question lies in the sovereignty of God and the response of His people, for, while revival involves the mysterious work of the Almighty One, when it comes it must begin in the house of the Lord and with the children of the Heavenly Father.

Repentance and sincere seeking of the face of God in prayer are hallmarks of the proper response of Christians to the urgent need for revival. J. Edwin Orr's classic trilogy on revival—*The Eager Feet, The Fervent Prayer, The Flaming Tongue*—powerfully documents this fact. And while Second Chronicles 7:14 ("If my people, who are called by my name, will humble themselves and pray and seek my face and turn from their wicked ways, then will I hear from heaven and will forgive their sin and will heal their land") was written to Israel, not America, the principle is valid, for "[r]ighteousness exalts a nation, but sin is a disgrace to any people" (Proverbs 14:34).

In His sovereign will, may God grant a mighty revival for His glory and the good of His, and all, people.

3. Declan McCullagh, "There's Something about Gary North," Wired News, January 7, 1999.

4. Quotations from various reconstructionists, throughout Chapter 1, "What Is Christian Reconstructionism?" in *Dominion Theology: Blessing or Curse?* by H. Wayne House and Thomas Ice (Portland, OR: Multnomah, 1988), 15-25.

5. Ibid., 7-10.

6. Ibid., 27.

7. Interview in the Prison Fellowship Newsletter, *Jubilee*, Summer 1999, 18.

8. Ibid., 21.

9. Ibid.

10. Ted Rendall, *Fire in the Church* (Burlington, ON: G.R. Welch Company Ltd., 1982), 28-29.

Chapter Fourteen

The Normal Christian Life

*[To be a Christian] means to be attached
to the Person of Christ, committed to the Lordship
of Christ and obedient to the commandments of Christ.*

—A.W. Tozer in *That Incredible Christian*

An incident in the life of a great man of faith from another era, the godly Andrew Murray, illustrates one of the characteristics of a true Christian. It is an essential mark of the only kind of person who will be able to respond in a truly biblical fashion to cultural collapse, a darkening world and the fearsome prospect of the fulfillment of end-time prophecy.

More Than Just a Decision

On one occasion an overnight guest in Andrew Murray's home came downstairs quite early in the morning to find his host seated at his desk, a Bible open before him. The candle beside him had burned low, and the guest remarked, "You've been up a long while."

"Yes," said Murray. "My Lord says, 'If you love Me, keep My commandments.' I do love Him, and so I've just been checking to see that I am keeping His commandments."

This declaration of a burning desire to obey the Word of the Lord is one of the clear evidences that a person has indeed become a child of God by faith. Such a relationship is the only adequate personal preparation for whatever difficult days may lie ahead for planet earth. More than this, it is an absolutely essential spiritual preparation if heaven is to be one's final home.

Unfortunately, in a great many instances in recent times, people have been urged simply to "decide for Christ" as though a mere intellectual choice of some sort can produce spiritual life. To be sure, entering into a relationship with Christ does involve the intellect and the will, but it is far more than just a decision.

We become members of the family of God only through the new birth.

Let's explore the biblical description of a genuine Christian life under the three aspects of such a life as indicated by A.W. Tozer in his definition from *That Incredible Christian.*[1]

First—Attached to the Person of Christ

Attachment to Christ is first and foremost. Without it no one can be a Christian. In fact, we become members of the family of God only through the new birth. Apart from the salvation which Christ alone provides, all of mankind is under God's just condemnation. The Bible makes that abundantly clear. "All have sinned; . . . there is no one righteous, not even one" (Romans 3:23, 10). And, "the soul who sins is the one who will die," for "the wages of sin is death" (Ezekiel 18:20; Romans 6:23). God's standard is perfection—He doesn't grade on a curve. There is no one who can measure up, for there is no one who hasn't sinned. That's the bad news. We're all doomed.

But there is good news: God does not want people to suffer the eternal death which sin's penalty demands (Ezekiel 18:23, 32). In His great love He has provided a way by which He can redeem man without violating His eternal decrees or His holy character. That way is through His Son, the Lord Jesus Christ.

Jesus was born of the virgin Mary, lived a sinless life and then died on the cross as the perfect substitute for sinful man. Though He was undeserving of death, He took sin's penalty in our place. And, because He is God, His payment is adequate for all humanity.

> For God so loved the world that he gave his one and only Son, that whoever believes in him shall not perish but have eternal life. For God did not send his Son into the world to condemn the world, but to save the world through him. Whoever believes in him is not condemned, but whoever does not believe stands condemned already because he has not believed in the name of God's one and only Son. (John 3:16-18)

Christ's resurrection was the documentation and declaration of His deity and victory over sin and death (1 Corinthians 15). Jesus declares, "I am the way and the truth and the life. No one comes to the Father except through me" (John 14:6). The Way has been provided by which sinful man can be forgiven, cleansed of sin and brought into a right relationship with God.

It is our responsibility and privilege to accept that Way, the Lord Jesus Christ. We become attached to Him as we acknowledge our sin, repent of it and in humble faith trust Christ's substitutionary death on the cross for our salvation.

How exactly does one do that?

The ABCs of Salvation

I have shared with thousands of people in person and hundreds of thousands more through my books what I call "The ABC Steps to Salvation." They are simple, but profound.

A—**Agree** with God and **Admit** that you are a lost sinner in need of salvation, that you cannot save yourself. Unless you are willing to acknowledge the bad news about yourself you cannot truly realize your need and come humbly to Christ.

B—**Believe** that the Lord Jesus Christ and He alone can save you (Acts 4:12). You must also believe that He *wants* to save you and that He *will* save you (John 5:24).

C—**Come** and **Call**. Jesus invites you to come to Him and promises that He will not turn away any who come (Matthew 11:28, John 6:37). The Bible also promises that whoever calls on the name of the Lord will be saved (Romans 10:13). To call on the Lord is simply to pray, admitting your lost condition and need of a Savior, expressing your faith that the Lord Jesus Christ alone can and will save you, and sincerely asking Him to forgive and cleanse you and give you eternal life.

If this has never been your experience, I urge you to take these steps now. Attachment to the Person of the Lord Jesus Christ as Savior is where and when the Christian life begins. But the normal Christian life, which begins with salvation, is far more than simply the assurance of heaven, as wonderful as that is. Salvation is only the start of a life lived under the authority of Christ.

Next—Committed to the Lordship of Jesus Christ

To yield to the lordship and control of Jesus Christ in one's life, even though it is how the normal Christian life is to be lived, is not natural. The inclination of all mankind, even Christians, is to want to be personally in control, to go one's own way (Isaiah 53:6). We all want to do our own thing.

Attachment to the Person of the Lord Jesus Christ as Savior is where and when the Christian life begins.

The Apostle Paul wrote in First Corinthians 12:3 that "no one can say 'Jesus is Lord,' except by the Holy Spirit." The implication is clear: the fullness of the Holy Spirit in a believer's life (and that alone) will enable him or her to declare and demonstrate the lordship of Christ in daily experience.

Therefore, to be filled with the Spirit is a command, not just a helpful suggestion, and applies to every believer, not just those in leadership. Ephesians 5:18—"Be filled with the Spirit"—is in the imperative voice, grammatically, meaning it is a command. Thus, since God has commanded it, and will give us whatever we ask for in His name, according to His will (Luke 11:11-13; 1 John 5:14-15), we can ask with assurance to be filled with the Holy Spirit.

The only prerequisites to experiencing Spirit-fullness are a cleansed life and a sincere desire. The next step is to ask in faith, and receive the filling of the Holy Spirit. Experience then the joy of Christian life as the Heavenly Father planned for it to be, which will include the third aspect of a normal Christian life: obedience.

Finally—Obedient to the Commands of Christ

It follows quite logically that if Jesus Christ is Lord—the supreme authority, the controller—in my life, I will want to be obedient to His commands.

It must be plainly stated here that obedience to the commands of the Lord is not to be undertaken in an effort to obtain salvation. Rather it is a by-product of salvation, a mark of love for the One who has already redeemed us and who is our Lord. Let there be no misunderstanding: salvation cannot be earned by any amount of obedience. Salvation is a free gift from God, offered in His love and mercy and received by faith. Obedience is a Spirit-enabled response of love and gratitude for that salvation.

The commandments of the Lord are not difficult to discover. They are clearly written throughout His Word, readily available for us to learn and do, in the power of His Spirit. That's the wonderful thing about our Master: He will not direct us to do something without providing the power to do it!

Getting on Track

If you have stuck with us to this point, you may be asking, "Where do I go from here?"

The answer is simple, though not easy. Just live the normal Christian life! Making certain, first, of your relationship to Christ and your surrender to the Holy Spirit, simply set yourself to discovering and obeying the commandments of the Lord on a daily basis.

You can trust the Holy Spirit to direct and enable you. He is the one who guides us into all truth (John 16:13). Perhaps begin with the Sermon on the Mount in Matthew chapters 5 through 7. Or read Romans, First and Second Corinthians, Philippians, Ephesians, all of which are instructive letters written to believers. Each of these Spirit-inspired epistles is full of direction from the Lord on life in the Spirit, fully applicable to this day and age. They're powerful and life-changing.

Judgment, Collapse—Is It Coming Soon?

As I confessed earlier, I am not a prophet.

I do not know what the future holds, and I make no predictions. As I've attempted to document in these pages, I do see that our culture is manifesting the characteristics of the final stage of an empire,[*] as history has revealed them to be.

I agree with the comment of Dr. Henry Blackaby, author of *Experiencing God*, when he responded to the question, "What do you see as the future for the United States?" His answer? "If you put the United States up against the Scriptures, we're in trouble. I think we're very close to the judgment of God."[2]

Whether or not we are close to the judgment of God, the collapse of the American Empire, and even of the empire of man, I cannot say. We may very well be. I can, however, say emphatically and without fear of being wrong, that wherever we may be on God's timetable for planet earth, as Christians we are to be salt and light. That demands that we genuinely know Christ as Savior and Lord and that we be committed to obeying His commandments in the power of His Spirit.

That is not a natural human response. It's supernatural.

To respond supernaturally will be a source of joy, both now and eternally.

My prayer is that such will be your response.

---

* Though our focus has been almost exclusively on the United States, similar characteristics are to be found in other nations of the world, such as Canada, Britain, European and other countries, and could just as easily be documented.

Endnotes

1. A.W. Tozer, *That Incredible Christian* (Camp Hill, PA: Christian Publications, 1998), 133.

2. Henry Blackaby, "Who Holds the Future?" *Current Thoughts & Trends*, January 2000, 2.

Epilogue

And He Shall Reign

During the writing of *When the Empire Strikes Out*, I took a break
from the almost total immersion in the project to enjoy a quiet
and very special Sunday in nearby Three Hills, Alberta, home of Prairie Bible College.

The highlight of the day, the first Sunday in Advent, was attending
an afternoon presentation of Handel's *Messiah* by a full orchestra and
200-voice choir drawn primarily from the student body of the college
and augmented by a few recruits from the community.

It was a delightful experience, like the beauty of brilliant sunshine
breaking through heavy, oppressive clouds on a dull, dark day, making
the world glorious with light!

Frankly, the intense research into the history of empires had been a
somewhat depressing experience for me. Actually, more than somewhat depressing—it had been downright depressing! I found it soul-
numbing to read and reflect upon account after account of seemingly
endless wars, with their multiplied millions of deaths through the
centuries.

It was difficult to consider the record of unspeakable and repeated
cruelty and brutality of man to man throughout history. The never-

ending accounts of murder, rape, pillage, intrigue and violence which fill the annals of our past served to dishearten and dismay. The staggering immorality and gross wickedness displayed in the final stages of empire after empire was mind-boggling and shocking to contemplate.

And what seemed even worse was the task of surveying our current culture with its ominous resemblance to the Age of Decline and Collapse in past empires. And, as we have sought to document, there does not appear to be much prospect in the immediate future of a break in the dark clouds on mankind's horizon—apart from divine intervention.

Individually, thank God, we can know Christ's presence, provision and protection, but for mankind in general, the future looks exceedingly bleak. Even the Rapture, a blessed event for the believer, will usher in the awesome Tribulation described in the Apocalypse.

Reflecting on these facts was weighing down my soul.

Then, like sun breaking through clouds, the glorious truths of Scripture, set to the powerful music of Handel, bathed my soul and spirit in celestial light with the reminders of God's sovereignty.

> For unto us a child is born,
> Unto us a son is given. . . .
> And the government shall be upon *His* shoulder . . .
> He is the *King* of glory.

Then, finally, the majestic soul-stirring "Hallelujah Chorus":

> Hallelujah! for the Lord God omnipotent reigneth . . .
> And *He shall reign* forever and ever.
> King of kings, and Lord of lords,
> Hallelujah! Hallelujah! Hallelujah!

Epilogue: And He Shall Reign

As I stood with that large audience during the rendition of the Chorus to honor the King Eternal, my heart soared, and I could not contain the tears of joy. I was reminded that He is, indeed, the Lord, the omnipotent Sovereign, the King of Kings. **HE SHALL REIGN!**

Later, as I reflected upon and basked in the truth that God is sovereign, that He is love and that we can trust the Judge of the whole earth to do right, the words of a Southern Gospel quartet song came to mind.

Ain't no need to worry
If you've been born again.
I've read the back of the Book
And we win!

That's a reassuring thought and a wonderful truth which will sustain us in whatever difficult days may lie ahead. However, if you've not been born again, that's not an assurance. For you, there is no decision in all of life as important as the decision to admit your need of a Savior, repent of your sin and trust Christ for salvation. Do it today.

In the meantime, for every believer, it's our responsibility and privilege to

- walk closely with our Lord in the power of His Spirit,
- hold loosely the things of earth, and
- make every effort to snatch loved ones, friends and neighbors from the fate that awaits all those who do not know Jesus Christ as their Lord and Savior.

In other words—live a normal Christian life.

Proclamation of President Bush's National Day of Prayer and Thanksgiving

(as reported in The Sunday Patriot-News, *Harrisburg, Pennsylvania, Sunday January 21, 2001)*

Nearly 200 years ago, on March 4, 1801, our young nation celebrated an important milestone in its history, the first transfer of power between political parties, as Thomas Jefferson took the oath of office as president. On this bicentennial of that event, we pause to remember and give thanks to Almighty God for our unbroken heritage of democracy, the peaceful transition of power and the perseverance of our government through the challenges of war and peace, want and prosperity, discord and harmony.

President Jefferson also wrote, "The God who gave us life gave us liberty at the same time," and asked, "Can the liberties of a nation be secure when we have removed a conviction that these liberties are of

God?" Indeed, it is appropriate to mark this occasion by remembering the words of President Jefferson and the examples of Americans of the past and today who in times of both joy and need turn to Almighty God in prayer. Times of plenty, like times of crisis, are tests of American character. Today, I seek God's guidance and His blessings on our land and all our people. Knowing that I cannot succeed in this task without the favor of God and the prayers of the people, I ask all Americans to join with me in prayer and thanksgiving.

Now, therefore, I, George W. Bush, president of the United States of America, by the authority vested in me by the constitution and laws of the United States, do hereby proclaim January 21, 2001, a National Day of Prayer and Thanksgiving and call upon the citizens of our nation to gather together in homes and places of worship to pray alone and together and offer thanksgiving to God for all the blessings of this great and good land. On this day, I call upon Americans to recall all that unites us. Let us become a nation rich not only in material wealth but in ideals—rich in justice and compassion and family love and moral courage. I ask Americans to bow our heads in humility before our Heavenly Father, a God who calls us not to judge our neighbors, but to love them, to ask His guidance upon our nation and its leaders in every level of government.

In witness whereof, I have hereunto set my hand this 20th day of January, in the year of our Lord 2001, and of the Independence of the United States of America the 225th.

Selected Bibliography

Adam, Alexander. *Roman Antiquities, or An Account of the Manners and Customs of the Romans.* New York: Collins, Keese & Co., 1836.

Alibek, Ken, with Stephen Handelman. *Biohazard.* New York: Random House, 1999.

Aries, Philippe and Duby, Georges, general editors. *A History of Private Life: From Pagan Rome to Byzantium.* Cambridge, MA & London: The Belknap Press of Harvard University, 1987.

Barna, George and Hatch, Mark. *Boiling Point: It Only Takes One Degree.* Ventura, CA: Regal Books, 2001.

Barron, Bruce. *Heaven on Earth? The Social and Political Agendas of Dominion Theology.* Grand Rapids, MI: Zondervan Publishing House, 1992.

Bernstein, Richard, and Munro, Ross H. *The Coming Conflict with China.* New York: Alfred A. Knoff, Inc., 1997.

Black, Jim Nelson. *When Nations Die, America on the Brink: Ten Warning Signs of a Culture in Crisis.* Wheaton, IL: Tyndale House Publishers, Inc., 1994.

Bork, Robert H. *Slouching Toward Gomorrah.* New York: Regan Books, 1996.

Cairns, Trevor, general editor. *Cambridge Introduction to the History of Mankind, Book 2, The Romans and Their Empire.* London: Cambridge University Press, 1970.

Carroll, John T. *Response to the End of History, Eschatology and Situation in Luke-Acts*. Atlanta, GA: Scholars Press, 1988.

Colby, Frank Moore. *Outlines of General History*. New York: American Book Co., 1899.

Colson, Charles. *Against the Night*. Ann Arbor, MI: Vine Books, Servant Publishers, 1989.

_____. *The Body, Being Light in the Darkness*. Dallas, TX: Word, 1992.

_____. *Kingdoms in Conflict*. Grand Rapids, MI: Morrow/Zondervan Publishers, 1987.

_____ and Pearcy, Nancy. *How Now Shall We Live*. Wheaton, IL: Tyndale House Publishers, Inc., 1999.

Durant, Will and Ariel. *The Story of Civilization: I Our Oriental Heritage*. New York: Simon and Schuster, 1935.

_____. *II The Life of Greece*, 1939.

_____. *III Caesar and Christ*, 1944.

_____. *IV The Age of Faith*, 1950.

_____. *V The Renaissance*, 1953.

_____. *VI The Reformation*, 1957.

_____. *VII The Age of Reason Begins*, 1961.

_____. *VIII The Age of Louis XIV*, 1963.

_____. *IX The Age of Voltaire*, 1965.

_____. *X Rousseau and Revolution*, 1967.

_____. *The Lessons of History*, 1968.

Bibliography

Erdoes, Richard. *A.D. 1000, Living on the Brink of Apocalypse.* New York: Harper Collins Publishers, Inc., 1988.

Feinberg, Charles L. *Millennialism, The Two Major Views.* Chicago, IL: Moody Press, 1980.

Forster, Roger T. and Marston, V. Paul. *God's Strategy in Human History.* Minneapolis, MN: Bethany House Publishers, 1973.

Garraty, John and Gay, Peter, general editors. *The Columbia History of the World.* New York: Harper and Row, Publishers, 1972.

Glubb, Sir John. *The Fate of Empires.* Edinburgh: William Blackwood & Sons, Ltd., 1981.

Gothard, Bill. *Be Alert to Spiritual Danger.* Wheaton, IL: IBYC, 1979.

Graham, Billy. *Storm Warnings.* Dallas, TX: Word, 1992.

_____. *Approaching Hoofbeats.* Waco, TX: Word, 1983.

Grant, Michael. *The Ancient Mediterranean.* New York: Penguin Books, 1969.

Gross, Martin L. *The End of Sanity.* New York: Avon Books, 1997.

Henry, Carl F. *Twilight of a Great Civilization, The Drift to Neo-Paganism.* Westchester, IL: Crossway Books, 1988.

Herman, Arthur. *The Idea of Decline in Western History.* New York: The Free Press, 1997.

Houellebeca, Michel. *The Elementary Particles.* New York: A.G. Knopf, 2000. (A novel, raunchy but powerful statement that the sexual [and other] revolution of the '60s and on has opened Pandora's box and will most certainly cause the end of our race.)

House, H. Wayne and Ice, Thomas. *Dominion Theology: Blessing or Curse?* Portland, OR: Multnomah, 1988.

Kennedy, Paul. *The Rise and Fall of the Great Powers.* New York: Vintage Books, 1989.

LaSor, William Sanford. *The Truth about Armageddon.* San Francisco: Harper & Row Publishers, 1982.

Lightner, Robert. *Last Days Handbook.* Nashville, TN: Thomas Nelson Publishers, 1997.

Lindsell, Harold. *The Gathering Storm.* Wheaton, IL: Tyndale House Publishers, 1980.

Lodge, Henry Cabot, editor-in-chief. *The History of Nations, Rome, Vol. III.* New York: P.F. Collins and Son, 1916.

Lutzer, Erwin. *Hitler's Cross.* Chicago, IL: Moody Press, 1995.

Poland, Larry W. *How to Prepare for the Coming Persecution.* San Bernardino, CA: Here's Life Publishers, 1990.

Preston, Richard. *The Cobra Event.* New York: Random House, 1997. This is a novel that apparently was read and reread by former President Clinton. It describes how bioterrorism could affect the U.S.

Rawlinson, George. *The Seven Great Monarchies of the Ancient Eastern World, Vol. II.* New York: A.L. Bert, Publisher, 1893.

Rendall, Ted S. *Fire in the Church.* Burlington, Ontario: G.R. Welch Company Limited, 1982.

Rosio, Bob. *The Culture War in America.* Lafayette, LA: Huntington House Publishers, 1995.

Ruggiero, Vincent R. *Warning: Nonsense Is Destroying America.* Nashville, TN: Thomas Nelson Publishers, 1994.

Bibliography

Schaeffer, Francis A. *How Should We Then Live? The Rise and Decline of Western Thought and Culture.* Old Tappan, NJ: Fleming H. Revell Co., 1976.

Scroggie, F. John. *The Divine Programme in Human History.* London: Pickering & Inglis, n.d.

Sommers, Christina Hoff. *The War Against Boys.* New York: Simon and Schuster, 2000.

Swenson, Richard A. *Hurtling Toward Oblivion, A Logical Argument for the End of the Age.* Colorado Springs, CO: Navigators Press, 1999.

Timperlake, Edward and Triplett, William C. II. *Red Dragon Rising.* New York: Regnery Publishing, Inc., 1999.

_____. *Year of the Rat.* New York: Regnery Publishing, Inc., 1998.

Toynbee, Arnold J. *A Study of History.* New York: Oxford University Press, 1947.

Tozer, A.W. *That Incredible Christian.* Camp Hill, PA: Christian Publications, 1998.

Trager, James. *The People's Chronology, A Year by Year Record of Human Events from Prehistory to the Present.* New York: Henry Holt and Company, 1992.

Walvoord, John F. *The Rapture Question.* Grand Rapids, MI: Zondervan Publishing House, 1974.

White, John Wesley. *Thinking the Unthinkable: Armageddon.* Lake Mary, FL: Creation House, 1992.

Scripture Index

Exodus

7-11 183

Deuteronomy

6:4-5, 17 195

1 Samuel

3:1 195
3:20 195
3:21 195
7:4 195

2 Chronicles

7:14 198

Psalm

2 180
2:6 180

Proverbs

14:34 198

Isaiah

9:6-7 180
11:6-10 180

Isaiah (cont.)

42:3-4 180
53:6 205
65:20-25 180

Jeremiah

3:17 180

Ezekiel

18:20, 23, 32 203
36-39 172

Daniel

7:24, 27 172
9:20-27 176
9:26-27 172
11:31-39 176
11:32-35 176
11:36-39 172
12:2 170
12:11 172

Joel

3:12-16 179

Zechariah

12:3 179
14:1-2 179
14:16 180

Matthew

5:13 171
5-7 206
11:28 204
22:30 182
24:15 . . . . 172, 176
24:15-24 177
25:31-46 179

Luke

11:11-13 205

John

3:16-18 203
5:24 204
6:37 204
14:6 203
16:13 206

Acts

4:12 204
17:31 190

Romans

3:10, 23 203
6:23 203
8:21-23 180
10:13 204
14:10-12 171

1 Corinthians

3:10-15 171
12:3 205
15 203
15:24-28 181
15:51-58 170

Ephesians

5:18 205

1 Thessalonians

4:14-18 170

2 Thessalonians

2:1-12 172
2:1-10 171
2:4 176
2:8 180
2:10 182

Titus

2:13 170

2 Peter

3:10-13 181

1 John

5:14-15 205

Revelation

6 173
6:2 173
6:3-4 173

Revelation (cont.)

6:5-6 174

6:7-8 174

6:9-11 174

6:12-17 174

7:3-8 171

7:9-14 177

8:1-2 174

8:7-13 175

9:1-12 175

9:13-21 . . . . 175, 176

9:16 141

11 182

11:1-12 172

11:3-13 . . . . 172, 177

12:1-17 176

13:1-18 . . . . 172, 176

13:5-17 179

13:11-17 172

13:15 177

14:1-5 177

14:6-7 . . . . 172, 179, 182

14:20 179

16 177

16:2 177

16:3 177

16:4 177

16:8-9 178

16:10-11 178

16:12 141

Revelation (cont.)

16:12-14 178
16:14-16 179
16:17-21 178
17 172
17:1-18 . . . . 172, 176
17:16-17 176
19:6-10 171
19:11-15 179
19:17-21 172
19:20 179
20:1-3 179
20:4-5 177
20:4-6 180
20:5-6 170
20:7-9 181
20:10 181
20:11-15 181
20:7-15 181
21:1-22:5 181

Subject Index

Abortion 36, 89, 124

Actors 24, 53, 54, 55, 95, 101, 110, 113

Affluence 19, 35, 62, 63, 64, 65, 67, 113, 116

Age of Outburst 15, 16, 23, 40, 41, 43

Age of Conquests 15, 16, 23, 40, 41, 43

Age of Commerce 15, 17, 23, 40, 41, 45

Age of Affluence 15, 18, 23, 40, 41, 45, 65, 67

Age of Intellect 15, 19, 20, 23, 40, 41, 45, 67-68

Age of Decadence 15, 20, 21, 24, 40, 41, 46

Age of Decline and Collapse 15, 22, 24, 40, 41, 46, 53,
                                                            55, 77, 127, 210

Alexander the Great 34, 35

Armageddon 178, 179, 219

America 27, 63, 73, 76, 110, 118, 122, 123, 124,
                                          125, 128, 129, 131, 132, 133, 137,
                                          139, 141, 151, 155, 198, 214

American Family Association 107, 111

Antichrist 172, 173, 176, 177, 178, 179

Arab Empire 15, 20

Barbarians 46, 126, 131, 133, 137, 138, 139, 153

Beatles 97

Billionaires 63

Bioterrorism 139, 140, 146

Bork, Robert 107, 111, 116, 117, 120, 121, 125,
127, 129, 130, 131, 132, 148, 215
Bowl Judgments 177
British Empire 3, 15, 197

Cato 52
Caesar 47
Celebrities 96, 98, 101
Chemical weapons 138, 146, 162
Chesterton, G.K.. 27
Christ 17, 168, 170, 172, 173, 179, 180,
182, 201, 202, 204, 205, 206, 211
Christianity 120, 191
Churchill, Winston 157
Chyna 97, 98
Clinton, Bill 93, 104
Clinton, Hillary 81, 84
Club of Rome 154, 163
Collapse 22, 50
Colson, Charles 25, 50, 51, 108, 114, 126,
127, 137, 153, 157, 187, 193
Commerce 17, 62
Communist China 141, 142, 145
Computer games 100
Conquest 16
Crime 119, 120, 125
Croft, Lara 101
Cyberwarfare 142, 143

Subject Index

Decadence 22, 50, 62

Decline and Fall of the Roman Empire, The 46, 55, 114, 156

Decline 22, 50

Defensiveness 50, 62, 69, 113

Dewey, John 68

Disney 4

Dobson, James 27, 128

Dominance of women 51, 62

"Doomsday bug" 147, 149

Douglas, Michael 65, 101-102

Durant, Will 30, 31, 32, 34, 35, 36, 39, 47, 51, 52,
53, 55, 61, 117, 126, 127, 133, 197

Education 19, 68, 69, 156, 160, 185, 189

Egalitarianism 126

Eminem 99

Exponentiality 160

Families 87

Family Research Council 124

Fate of Empires 11, 13

Feminist 82, 86, 87, 88, 89

Feminization of military 71

Frivolity 114, 116, 156

Fukuyama, Francis 154

Gates, Bill 4, 44, 63, 64

Gibbon, Edward 46, 114, 156

Gladitorial games 54

Global Trends 2015 . . . . 137, 146

Glubb, Sir John 7, 9, 10, 11, 13, 14, 15, 16, 17, 18, 19,
20, 21, 22, 23, 24, 25, 26, 27, 28, 31, 34,
36, 40, 41, 43, 50, 52, 53, 55, 57, 59, 62, 67,
69, 73, 76, 77, 78, 79, 90, 113, 124, 127

God 2, 50, 89

Graham, Billy 167, 169, 190

Great White Throne 181

Greece 35, 50

"Hallelujah Chorus" 210

Hannibal 26, 42

Heroes 23, 52, 62, 78, 93, 94, 95, 96,
97, 100, 101, 104, 109, 110, 113

Hitler 3

Hollywood 105, 108

Holy Spirit 168, 171, 172, 196, 205, 206

Hurtling Toward Oblivion 159, 162-163

Illegal aliens 76

Illegitimacy 124, 125

Immigration 50, 62, 74, 75, 113

Individualism 126

Intellect 19

Israel 10, 133, 168, 172, 178, 179, 195, 196, 197, 198

Jesus Christ 118, 168, 179, 181, 196, 203, 204, 206, 211

Judah 196

Subject Index

Lethality 161, 162
Lodge, Henry Cabot 46, 49, 104

Macedonian Empire 16
Madonna 64, 65, 104, 107
Mark Anthony 47
Maples, Marla 108
Median Empire 28
Microsoft 4, 63, 65
Military. 10, 71, 72, 73, 123
Millennium. 138, 180, 182, 185
Mongol Empire 17
Monroe, Marilyn 64, 104
Murray, Andrew 201

Nero 48
New Establishment 68, 74, 76, 83, 84
New Jerusalem. 181

Patriotism 19
Persian Empire 31, 32
Pornography 120, 121, 122, 160
President Bush 108, 196, 213, 214
Profusion. 159

Radical egalitarianism 126, 129, 130, 131
Radical individualism 126, 129, 130, 131
Rapture 170, 171, 182, 188, 189, 210

Rawlinson, George 28, 29, 30
Reclusivism 189
Reconstructionism 189, 198
Reagan, Ronald 1
Religion 120, 171, 173
Restorationism 189
Revival 194, 195
Revivalism 189, 194
Rodriquez, Alex 102
Roman Antiquities 44, 53
Roman Empire 17, 27, 28, 37, 40, 41, 42, 46, 55, 131
Russia 23, 69, 70, 133, 157, 158, 172

Satan 172, 179, 180, 181
Schaeffer, Francis 27, 39, 218
Schweitzer, Albert 155
Seal judgments 173, 175, 176, 177
Sexuality 39, 124
Shopping 67
Singers 24, 53, 101
Slouching Toward Gomorrah 111, 116, 148, 215
Star Wars 1, 2
Story of Civilization, The 30, 55, 126, 197
Supreme Court 118, 131
Super Bowl 96
Swenson, Richard 159, 160, 161, 162

Terrorist 137, 138, 139
Tolstoy 115
Toynbee, Arnold 28, 32, 33, 56

Subject Index

Tozer, A.W.. . . . . 201, 202
Tribulation 173, 174, 179, 182, 210
Trumpet Judgments 175, 176, 177

U.N. 89, 91

Ventura, Jesse 103
Violent crime 119, 120
Virtue 19, 95

Washington, George 104
Wealth. 18, 43, 68
Weapons of mass destruction. 139, 162
Welfare 50-51, 62, 77, 78, 87, 113, 125
Wesley, John. 197
Winfrey, Oprah 99
Witches 88
Wolfe, Alan 74
Women, dominant 51, 78, 113
World Wrestling Federation. 96

Zeta-Jones, Catherine 65, 107

Books by William R. Goetz

Apocalypse Next

UFOs: Friend, Foe or Fantasy?

The Economy to Come

Once upon a Christmas

Once upon an Easter

When the Empire Strikes Out